WHAT IS IT ABOUT ME YOU CAN'T TEACH?

AN INSTRUCTIONAL GUIDE FOR THE

URBAN EDUCATOR

ELEANOR RENEÉ RODRIGUEZ
& JAMES BELLANCA

SkyLight

TRAINING AND PUBLISHING, INC.

Arlington Heights, Illinois

Grateful acknowledgment is made to the following for use of copyrighted works:

"To the Young Who Want to Die" by Gwendolyn Brooks, from *Near Johannesburg Boy*, © 1987, courtesy of Third World Press, Chicago.

"The Funeral of Martin Luther King Jr." by Nikki Giovanni, from *Black Feeling, Black Talk, Black Judgement* by Nikki Giovanni, © 1968, 1970 courtesy of William Morrow and Co., Inc.

What Is It about Me You Can't Teach? An Instructional Guide for the Urban Educator

Published by IRI/SkyLight Training and Publishing, Inc.
2626 S. Clearbrook Dr., Arlington Heights, IL 60005-5310
800-348-4474 or 847-290-6600
Fax 847-290-6609
info@iriskylight.com
http://www.iriskylight.com

Creative Director: Robin Fogarty
Managing Editor: T. B. Zaban
Editor: Edward Roberts
Graphic Designer: Bruce Leckie
Formatter: Heidi Ray
Type Composer: Donna Ramirez
Cover Designer: David Stockman
Production Supervisor: Bob Crump

LCCCN 96-78752
ISBN 0–57517-066-3

1494E-7-98V
Item Number 1444
06 05 04 03 02 01 00 99 98   15 14 13 12 10 9 8 7 6 5

In loving memory
of one of our many
"Boys 'n the Hood"
who lost his life needlessly—
my nephew
Razell McCoy
September 23, 1976—February 15, 1995

Eleanor Reneé Rodriguez

Contents

Foreword

On too few occasions does one have an opportunity to read a book which approaches the most important questions regarding student achievement and school reform. *What Is It about Me You Can't Teach?* by Eleanor Reneé Rodriguez and Jim Bellanca is a book which faces the domain given short shrift in the nation's analysis of what is going wrong with many schools, i.e., the importance of preparing and keeping good teachers. Though a recent national publication by Linda Darling-Hammond, *What Matters Most: Teaching for America's Future*, addresses the centrality of teaching and learning and its impact on achievement, very few school reform publications give attention to the issue of classroom instruction.

Rodriguez and Bellanca have made an important contribution to the school reform literature. In this book they acknowledged (through the "voices of children") the impact that teacher attitudes and performance have on the learning of the urban child. Poignant examples abound here, which force the reader to consider how teachers behave differently to many urban students. As has been reported by the authors in their examples, teachers often tend to slow down the pace of learning, persist less strenuously in helping students, and view urban children as disadvantaged, unruly, unsocialized, slow, and backward—thus perpetuating a self-fulfilling prophecy. Teachers who expect students to be successful will work toward that end, and usually they will produce results that justify their optimism, e.g., providing strategies which deliver subject matter in interesting ways and helping the students to cognitively adapt and process information.

The legacy of research from the eighties and nineties is that urban teachers must change their teaching practices in the direction of concentrating more time and effort on concept and cognitive development, reasoning, thinking, and higher-order comprehension skills when engaged in subject-matter instruction. A strong base of research linking cognitive development to prior knowledge in learning emerged in the late 1970s. Those studies concluded that, particularly when reading is the learning mode, those students with much prior knowledge and experience relevant to a subject have less difficulty learning new material and retain more than those with inadequate or incomplete prior knowledge and experiences. Urban students need the benefit of teachers who know how to access prior knowledge that students might not be aware of and that might help them with the material to be learned.

Through illustrative examples, Rodriguez and Bellanca guide the reader through integrated and interdisciplinary lessons that use much of the cognitive research referred to above. The reader is guided on a virtual tour of relevant topics and ideas which will work well with all students, but particularly with urban children. The use of predictions, graphic organizers, elements of Feuerstein's Instrumental Enrichment Program, concept themes, problem-solving strategies, and concept attainment models are all embedded in content-area instruction. This synthesis provides the conceptual foundation necessary for appropriate classroom mediation.

The lasting contribution of this book is that it also gives the reader a clear portrait of the educator best able to serve urban students. This educator is sensitive, empathetic, confident, knowledgeable about appropriate teaching methodologies and subject-matter, and is acclimated to the nuances of learning used by many urban children. This educator also provides a strong role model for the students, maintains high expectations for all students served, and is able to integrate academic learning into structured applied learning opportunities. Thus, the context of schooling becomes one of nurturance, guidance, leadership and support, in spite of the harsh realities of everyday life continually faced by many urban students in our schools.

I am pleased to introduce this book to our many partners in urban school systems across the country and to thank the authors for their outstanding contribution.

Eric Cooper
National Urban Alliance for Effective Education
Teachers College, Columbia University, New York

IRI/Skylight Training and Publishing, Inc.

Acknowledgments

The framework for this book is based on Reuven Feuerstein's seminal work with the mediated learning experience (MLE). Especially helpful are Reuven's ten criteria for high quality mediation. These criteria served as the major guide for linking the many strategies and structures to each other and to their meaningful use in the classroom.

Additional acknowledgments must be made to those who encouraged this work. Appreciation must be expressed to Julie Noblitt for her invaluable assistance and encouragement. Every now and then she may have felt as though she were in a lions' den, trying to pull teeth during our status meetings. She was able to come out of the meeting saying "We made progress!" with a smile on her face.

And finally, to my friends and family, specifically my hero, husband, and friend, Joseph H. Rodriguez, who hung in there and repeatedly encouraged me to tie a knot at the end of my rope and keep on hanging until this project was complete. I am thankful.

A Special Note

A wise man knows a proverb reconciles difficulties.

—Yoraba

Storytelling in Africa is an important oral tradition, and each story contains a lesson which highlights history, customs, and/or traditions. I love African proverbs. To me, they are the short and concise means to an end. Like the Nigerian proverb, "It takes a village to raise a child," is remembered and used as a way to tell it: it takes everyone to educate everyone. Proverbs or sayings are used throughout this book in places where emphasis or additional attention is needed to reinforce a point. Enjoy!

Introduction

Andrea remembers the day it happened. "I was sitting in geography class. I was a sophomore. The day had started out really bad. My mother was on my case for my bad grades. My teacher was handing back our tests. When he got to me, he threw the test on the desk. All I saw were the red marks. 'Your kind,' he said, 'don't deserve a desk.' I didn't even hear what else he had to say. I snapped. Just snapped when I heard that 'your kind.' It was the last straw. I didn't say anything when he ignored my raised hand or all the times he pretended I wasn't there. When I snapped, I just glared and said in my meanest voice, 'Mr. Rossi, just what is it about me you can't teach?'"

■ The Challenge of Urban Education

Many urban teachers struggle to keep aging walls graffiti-free, work with textbooks bound together with tape, and labor to keep students safe from wayward bullets and drug-dealing miscreants.

Andrea's angry question brought into the open the issue central to teaching and learning in urban classrooms: the nature of what teachers bring with them in dealing with their diverse student populations. Teachers in the affluent suburban schools have well-equipped classrooms and laboratories, extensive counseling and tutorial services in place, up-to-date textbooks, community support programs, extensive extracurricular programs, and cutting-edge technology at their disposal. Many urban teachers struggle to keep aging walls graffiti-free, work with textbooks bound together with tape, and labor to keep students safe from wayward bullets and drug-dealing miscreants. More often than not, the urban teacher who cares about making a difference buys her own supplies, counsels troubled children, resolves intense physical and verbal conflicts, and invents ways to include special challenge students for whom no other resources are provided. Working in an ER trauma center or air traffic control tower may seem like a dreamland compared to working inside an urban classroom.

■ Reform Efforts

Aided by the national reform movement begun with *A Nation at Risk*, there has been a plethora of organized reform efforts in urban school districts. Legislators, parents, teachers' organizations, professional educators' organizations, community agencies, and universities have joined the movement. From these efforts have come national standards, alternative and charter schools, site-based management, community service agency–school collaboration, public and parental engagement, teacher empowerment, choice plans, professional development schools, financial rewards for school-based improvement, lengthened school days, state takeovers, and privatization.

This book is not about any of those efforts. It makes no judgment about which of these efforts help or don't help urban students. What we do here is address the great, unforgotten, and often ignored issue of high quality instruction in the urban classroom. Most teachers and most students are made, not born. Some students may be born with more natural ability than others to calculate, to read, to interact with others, or to excel at sports, but most learn how to succeed through the sweat of their brows and the sweat of their teachers' brows. In like manner, some teachers are born with more ability to motivate learning than others, but most improve how they teach through hard work and advanced study. Thus, just as all children can learn to function in school more successfully through their own intense work and the skills of their teachers, so too all teachers can learn to teach more skillfully. Every basketball player is not Michael Jordan, but Michael Jordan didn't become a great player without developing his talents; every person who writes a poem is not a Maya Angelou, but Maya Angelou didn't become a great poet by neglecting her natural talent. Basic ability in children is not a limit but a starting place. The same is true of teachers.

This book focuses on research conducted in the last twenty years that shows what a teacher can do to add new knowledge and skills to her repertoire of teaching talent so that her students can increase their own talents and achievements. Because the book deals with the environment of the urban school, it gives tighter focus to what the research suggests will most help the urban classroom teacher.

This book focuses on research that will help the urban classroom teacher.

What happens with instruction in the urban classroom does not negate the importance of those reform efforts which in fact help make productive teaching more likely; good instruction alone will not save our schools. However, all of the reform efforts are tangential to the central issue: the need for one hundred percent attention and improvement of instruction. Instruction, connected with a meaningful curriculum and sound assessment, are the most essential ingredients. Without improvement in instruction, there will be no improvement in student achievement and no development of student talents.

☐ Student Achievement and Teacher Expectations

Most of the research on student achievement asserts that improvement begins with the expectations of the classroom teacher. This book is not addressed to teachers in urban classrooms who believe that there is nothing they can do to improve their students' learning performance. Please don't scoff at the seriousness of the issue. The fact that such beliefs permeate urban schools is not to be minimized. For instance, at a recent meeting of high school mathematics teachers from a large urban system, in a room dominated by a bulletin board imprinted with the motto "We Believe All Can Learn—So Go For It," the responses to the question "How do we get more than sixty percent of our students to pass the state finals?" illustrate how subtle and deep are the low expectations held by the teachers:

>"Get their parents involved."

>"Get them to do more homework."

>"Weed them out sooner."

>"You can't teach lazy folks."

>"Most belong in special education."

>"They can't think."

IRI/SkyLight Training and Publishing, Inc.

"It's a dead-end street."

"They don't care. They don't have important goals."

These comments, delivered by a mixture of African American, Hispanic, and Caucasian teachers, experienced and skilled in the teaching of mathematics, show frustration and the belief that nothing could be done for the forty percent who were failing the test. These teachers' low expectations and ironclad vision—that students of the poor, students of color, students with special challenges, or students who speak other languages cannot learn—will continue to hold true. These students will not learn because they are not expected to learn, they were "excused" from learning, and they are instructed in ways that guarantee that they will not learn.

However, this book *is* addressed to teachers who *do* believe that all children can learn. Some of these teachers have great natural ability to teach all children, including urban children with diverse backgrounds, children with special challenges, and children with little wealth. These teachers are the Michael Jordans, the Maya Angelous, and the Martin Luther King Jrs. of the teaching profession. Most teachers, however, know they must continue to develop their talents and find ways to put the words "all children can learn" into practice. Many perform well without being superstars; but they do want all children to learn. They work in districts with the poorest classroom resources spread thinly among many challenged youngsters; they often have the least opportunity for the professional development which will help them learn about "best practice," the most recently discovered methods and alternative instructional strategies. Their motto is "Yeah, we do believe all children can learn"—their question is "How?"

"Yeah, we do believe all children can learn —the question is, How?"

Teaching in the modern urban classroom may be the most difficult challenge in the most difficult profession, but it also provides the greatest opportunity for a teacher to make a difference. Our focus here is on the knowledge that will help those committed to teaching any children who enter their classrooms.

In this book are hundreds of practical strategies for immediate implementation. Some of the approaches to learning that are described here will require more practice and support over a longer period. These are balanced by sample lesson designs that delineate how to couple effective practices with course content and assessment in a lesson or unit design that will have the most impact on students. All of these are described in the context of research that shows how each approach is effective in urban classrooms. However, there is a "caveat," a "beware." All the instructional approaches are described with the forewarning that no single approach will help in every classroom every time. Each practice needs judicious decision making on the teacher's part. The teacher will make the chosen strategy appropriate for the content, the students' needs, and the situation. As the urban teacher selects the appropriate strategy, she will make it an important part of her repertoire, her toolkit of approaches, that she will apply more and more skillfully as she grows in experience. With successful application of the tools will come the proof that indeed all children, including the much-maligned urban children, can learn because she, their teacher, has the tools, the talent, and the commitment to make it happen.

■ Urban Children and the Challenges They Face

The development of a classroom teacher is a lifelong journey. An integral part of that journey is understanding the children in the classroom. As urban teachers progress on their journey, it is important to review the four main characteristics of the urban child. Who is the urban child? What are the truths and what are the myths?

The Urban Child

One of the main problems encountered in educating urban children is the speed with which they are expected to grow up.

The first thing to know is that the urban child is a human being between the ages of birth and eighteen. Often, when referring to young adults receiving special education services, the age is extended to twenty-one. These ages generally encompass the early childhood primary, intermediate, junior or middle, and high school grades. Although it is becoming more difficult to recognize pre-teens and teenagers as children nowadays, they are still children. In fact, one of the main problems encountered in educating urban children is the speed with which they are expected to grow up. Urban children are having more intense and different life experiences as children than most adults have had. These types of experiences can, and more than likely will, physically and psychologically age anyone. However, chronologically, the urban child, or any child for that matter, is still a child, regardless of the number or types of experiences.

Victims of Labels

Second, the urban child (the adjective used to be "inner city") is likely to be, more than most children, a victim of labels which communicate and allow low expectations. The list on the following page covers excuses that teachers, principals, social workers, parents, and even the children themselves use to escape the challenge of rigorous learning and the assistance of strong instruction. More often than not, the labels are preceded in very subtle ways by some other phrase that is the heart and soul of low expectations.

"I can't teach you because you are . . ."

black

brown

yellow

red

white

of interracial
background

a Chapter 1/
Title I student

not a native English
speaker

bilingual

monolingual

Limited English
Proficient

a free lunch student

a reduced lunch
student

a neighborhood walker

a latch-key kid

an oldest child

a youngest child

a middle child

an only child

fatherless

motherless

homeless

federally connected

a left brain learner

a right brain learner

without a brain

of low SES (socio-
economic status)

of high SES

from a rural area

from an urban area

from a suburban area

learning disabled

visually impaired

orthopedically
handicapped

speech impaired

emotionally disordered

attention deficit-
hyperactivity
disordered

autistic

hearing impaired

lesbian

gay

dyslexic

a hemophiliac

medically fragile

asthmatic

hyperactive

overactive

inactive

slow

backward

basic

a nonreader

illiterate

an underachiever

a gifted
underachiever

a migrant

a transient

"at-risk"

a "jail bird"

a ward of the state

an orphan

an adoptee

a truant

the child of middle-aged
parents

HIV positive

not immunized

a drop out

born after
September 18

not ready for
kindergarten

a Headstart recipient

a food stamp recipient

a welfare recipient (Aid
to Families with
Dependent Children—
AFDC)

a WIC (Women, Infants,
and Children) program
participant

a public housing resident

a Section 8 resident

physically abused

sexually abused

a head trauma victim

wheelchair-bound

paralyzed

afflicted with Down's
syndrome

behaviorally disturbed

emotionally disturbed

educationally deficient

educationally
handicapped

IRI/SkyLight Training and Publishing, Inc.

Students Meeting Low Expectations

Third, the urban child is the individual (especially when male) most likely to end up in prison. How does this occur? Consider two examples that trace part of the responsibility to low-expectation practices in a school.

Abdul played his way through middle school. With twenty-two days of truancy his previous year, a failure in PE and Industrial Arts, and barely passing grades in his academics, Abdul ended up with a basic high school schedule for ninth grade: Practical Math, Basic English, Data Entry, Wood Shop, and General Science. After the first week of classes, Abdul told his sister that he was done with school (Abdul's mother was dead, his father lived out of state). Upset, the sister dragged Abdul into the counselor's office. After hearing the sister's complaints about Abdul's schedule and noting recorded remarks from teachers such as "You are in Data Entry so you can get a job where you can succeed," "This is your fifth time through this basic math, I hope you get it this time," and "Stupid is as stupid does—this class is for the most stupid," the counselor commented, "Look, he's obviously not able to do this minimum work—if he could, he'd be in class now. We're doing the best we can. But he has to be able to do the work."

At this point, Abdul's sister pulled a copy of Abdul's test record from her pocket. Under IQ she pointed to the number 147. The counselor, stunned only for a moment, said, "This can't be Abdul's. No kids in this school ever got that score."

Abdul left school the next month. Three years later, he was in prison. The ability he was thought not to have appeared in his street activities. Within a month of going fulltime to the streets, he became an accountant—organizing the books for his 450-member gang that specialized in crack sales totaling millions of dollars per year.

Jose's experience was no better. A gifted athlete who played on the all-city, all-star team in the sixth grade, he was turned down from admission to the junior high Spanish class. When he asked why, the principal responded, "You people are good athletes, but you'll never cut it in a language class." Five years later, Jose received a twenty-year sentence. His crime? Jose had become a skilled forger, earning several hundred thousand dollars for his gang each year.

Children of Single Parents

Fourth, the urban child is likely to be the child with a single parent, who is most likely female and most likely trapped in a low-pay, dead-end job or else fighting to survive on welfare. Many teachers who work in the urban schools look at this parent and make superficial judgments, and these judgments translate to low expectations:

"How can you expect Mario to do better? His father is in the state pen."

IRI/SkyLight Training and Publishing, Inc.

"Her mother didn't even finish grade eight. Where does she think she's going?"

"Antonio's mother never comes to school. She doesn't care."

The Task Ahead

Sadly, the stories of urban children who are expected to fail are quite common. Whether the abuse they experience comes from teachers' true belief about the students' abilities or because the teachers lack the know-how to work with these students, the students themselves will never know. If teachers are struggling to find fresh, practical approaches, we believe that the material that follows will provide a new, positive direction for them and their students.

Many teachers working in urban schools make superficial judgments about single parents.

CHAPTER 1

High Expectations

They expected nothing,
gave little, and got the
same in return.

—Charlayne Hunter-Gault
Resurrection City,
Washington, DC, 1968

Everybody says it: "All children can learn." But what do they mean? Some qualify their statements by saying, "All children can learn, providing. . ." Others say, "All children, except for . . .". Still others add various phrasings of "if," "but," and "when" in order to qualify the statement.

◻ All Children Can Learn

The sentiment "all children can learn" is a popular declaration. The practices that make the sentiment a reality are not so readily demonstrated in urban classrooms, though. The scarcity of these practices says more about the lack of conviction behind the espoused belief than it does about the sentiment itself. When the discrepancy between the "talk" and the "walk" is noted, the conversation turns quickly to excuses, rationales, and other evasions as defenses for explaining why it is that "these children" can't be taught.

Happily, there are many educators who do talk the talk and walk the walk. They have found many ways to put their unqualified belief into successful practice. Just as Henry Higgins followed his words with actions when he transformed Eliza Doolittle from a street-talking flower girl into a polished socialite who fooled the experts, so too many educators work to transform all their students, including those who present the most significant learning challenges, into active, engaged, and successful learners.

The belief that "all children can learn" springs from the positive point of view about learning potential. When the pessimists look at children and see the glass half empty, they go into a blue funk. "See," they say, "these children have limited intelligence. According to the statistics graphed on the bell curve, people with limited intelligence contribute the least to our gross national product and the most to crime and to welfare. Education, then, does no good." On the other hand, the optimist looks at the glass and sees that it is half full. "There is much we can do," they beam. "It may take more work, but let us use the best tools we have to educate each child to the fullest." Unlike pessimists such as Jensen, Murray, and Hartenstein, the optimists know that solid research supporting their view does exist.

In the last two decades, the optimists have demonstrated that there are strategies for dispelling the myths that only those measured to be bright or those who are given strong early education at home can learn. Two of these optimists, Samuel Kermin, director of the Teacher Expectations and Student Achievement (TESA) project for the Los Angeles County School System, and Reuven Feuerstein, the Israeli cognitive psychologist who created Instrumental Enrichment, have made especially valuable contributions. More recent contributions include Gardner's theory of multiple intelligences and the growing movement toward authentic learning and assessment.

Colorism, like colonialism, sexism, and racism, impedes us.
—Alice Walker,
In Search of Our Mother's Garden (1993)

◻ TESA

In the mid-seventies, Samuel Kermin and the Los Angeles County School Board introduced the results of a multi-year study, TESA. Having reviewed the early research on how teacher behavior influenced student performance, Kermin and his associates devised practical means for teachers of poor and minority students, long thought of as impossible to teach, in order to help "all children learn." Kermin and his associates identified fifteen teacher behaviors that seemed to have the greatest impact on how students improved their performance on reading and mathematics testing and created a training program to enable teachers to practice the belief. For the first time on a large public scale, the TESA program demonstrated what it takes to transform the belief into a reality. High expectations, as implemented through the fifteen teacher behaviors, showed that poverty and race were not insuperable barriers to learning. The real barriers were created by the low-level expectations with which these children were taught. With new teacher behaviors, substantive learning was as possible for these children as for the children of affluence and influence.

Following the initial success of TESA with the children of Los Angeles County, Kermin and his associates designed and disseminated a teacher-training program, now universally known as TESA, to expand the impact of the initial research. In this training program they outlined the research on each of the behaviors, modeled how a teacher might effectively implement each behavior, conducted guided practice, and set up coaching teams to provide classroom observation and on-the-spot feedback.

Following the lead provided by the "the wait-time lady," Mary Budd Rowe, and by Robert Rosenthal's study "Pygmalion in the Classroom," the TESA program's studies showed how selected teaching behaviors such as wait-time, proximity, higher-order questions, and constructive feedback were missing in classrooms where the teachers lacked the belief that all children can learn. Most notably, the researchers found that teachers behaved differently toward students that they believed had low learning ability. Most often, these judgments were based on stereotypes of class, race, and family. For these children, the teachers asked low-order, factual questions such as "Who is the main character?" or "What year did Columbus sail from Spain?" or else asked them to choose the correct answer to fill in a blank. When teachers perceived children to be slow, they used less wait time, reinforced correct responses less, and provided less individual attention.

On the other hand, the TESA researchers noted changes in behavior when teachers believed that certain children had the capability for high performance. For these children, the teachers were more likely to make regular and consistent use of the high expectations behaviors. For these students, a teacher was more likely to ask a question that required the student to think ("Why do you think that Lincoln freed the slaves?"), wait more than five seconds for the student's response, and provide positive and expansive feedback ("That was an excellent answer. I especially liked your inclusion of the description of the political pressure . . .").

Researchers found that teachers behaved differently toward students that they believed had low learning ability.

IRI/SkyLight Training and Publishing, Inc.

Kermin and his associates demonstrated that once teachers were provided with new ways to interact with students for whom they held low expectations, the teachers themselves would interact differently with those students. The students, challenged to respond in new ways, would improve their own performance and behavior in the classroom. In a sense, the new teaching behaviors forced a different type of teacher-student interaction. The new interactions resulted in the students' responding in more positive ways. The students' responses changed the teachers' perceptions of what their students could do and learn. The more the teachers changed how they taught, the more they transformed students into engaged learners. For instance, when low-expectations teachers ignored misbehavior, non-compliance with task instructions, failure to complete tasks, or exhibition of "who cares?" behavior, or when they merely shouted and screamed at the students, they saw instant but short-lasting changes in the students. Compliance was swift but disappeared once the sound and fury was over. When these teachers—who had once argued vociferously in defense of their scream-and-punish tactics—learned how to use cues, higher-order questioning, wait time, and the other TESA strategies, they saw new, lasting results with their students. Buoyed by the positive responses, the teachers increased praise, proximity, and other reinforcers that resulted in additional positive responses. Indeed, Kermin's hypothesis about high expectation practices proved that changed teacher behavior could change student performance.

TESA's success had a major impact on how educators thought about poor and minority students. First, the project demonstrated clearly that teachers' high and low expectations directly affect the learning of children. Second, the project developed a systematic method that enabled teachers to revise their low expectations in favor of high expectation behaviors. Third, the project destroyed the myth of the "natural" teacher that had dominated American education. The project's results made a solid argument for improving the quality of teacher training and development, improvements that would provide teachers with successes in teaching and transform their attitudes about student potential for learning. This in turn would fuel additional successes in their work with at-risk children. Fourth, the project provided easy-to-use, easy-to-learn teaching tools that produced strong, measurable, and significant results in the achievement level of students often claimed to be "unmotivated" or "not teachable." Finally, the project demonstrated how poverty, family history, and race are too easily used as excuses by educators who get low-performance results from students, largely because they teach with low expectations beliefs and strategies.

Children respond to the expectations of their environment.
—William Grier and Price Cobb
Black Rage
(1968)

◨ Mediated Learning

At the same time that Kermin was working with TESA, Reuven Feuerstein was paralleling the TESA successes with a very different approach in Israel. Having studied with Piaget in France, Feuerstein developed a system of learning for the children of the Holocaust who arrived in Israel from all parts of the world following World War II. Working in Kibbutz schools, Feuerstein faced the challenge of teaching children devastated by concentration camp life and the near destruction of their families and cultures. The children had come from the deserts of Ethiopia, the fields of Lebanon, and the ravaged nations of Europe and Asia. Few brought formal learning with them; many brought the remnants of emotional devastation and cognitive deficits. Most lacked what Feuerstein called "the prerequisites of learning."

Feuerstein found that his special students lacked "the prerequisites of learning."

When placed in the classrooms of the Kibbutzim, these children caused their teachers to throw up their hands and declare, "You are impossible to teach, you cannot learn!" What the teachers experienced were children and young adults whose impulsive behavior, inability to connect information, and passivity blocked all attempts at formal schooling.

Rather than deny the perceptions of these experienced teachers, Feuerstein, a classic optimist, saw that the "jars were half-filled. I knew from my diagnoses that these were giant jars. We had much to do, but we were not sure how to do it." In his commitment to find ways to open "these minds locked and chained against learning," Feuerstein adapted traditional IQ assessment instruments to the task of discovering why these children functioned so poorly. After all, he noted, they had survived far more serious threats to life and limb before getting to Israel. Using his collection of test tools, which he later named "Learning Propensity Assessment Devices." Feuerstein identified fourteen cognitive functions which were prerequisites for significant achievement. Comparing the early childhood experiences of his special students with students who were having success in school, he found that the children who were struggling lacked the prerequisites. In addition, Feuerstein found that parents were the primary providers of the "mediation" that developed these prerequisites. Because the war and the camps had so destroyed their families, the children Feuerstein was attempting to assist had never experienced the necessary mediation.

Having identified the problem, Feuerstein next faced the challenge of finding the possibilities for introducing the weak cognitive functions that could give older children the cognitive foundations they had missed. These investigations led to the development of his theory of mediated learning and the instructional practices which made the theory work.

The theory of mediated learning begins with the presupposition that all children can learn. For Feuerstein, there are no qualifications to this belief.

There are only the limits imposed by those who desire excuses to avoid the challenge of mediating success for all.

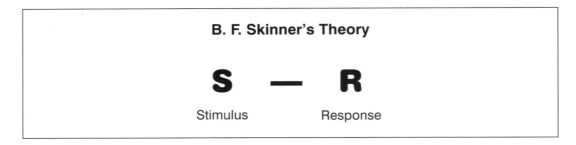

B. F. Skinner's Theory

S — R

Stimulus   Response

Feuerstein's systematic approach to teaching and learning begins with a rejection of Skinner's behavior modification theory, with its belief that learning is merely a response to external stimuli. Taking his cue from Piaget, Feuerstein teaches that learning springs from within the individual's heart and mind. Without internal motivation there is no learning for humans.

Piaget introduced the concept that the teacher's major role is the creation of a rich learning environment appropriate to the student's cognitive development. In this scenario, later expanded by Vygotsky in his early explanation of idea construction, the learner makes "meaning" from stimuli provided by the teacher in the classroom. Feuerstein also adopted the belief that learning is centered in the active mental engagement of the learner with past knowledge and new experiences. In this engagement process, the learner melded new with old, and the result was "learning."

Feuerstein parted ways with Vygotsky, however. Feuerstin postulated that the best quality of learning does not occur in an environmental vacuum. He noted how parents, siblings, and other significant individuals can impact the learner from the earliest years. He also noted that many children, denied this interaction by poverty, racism, or other negative environmental conditions, failed to develop their learning capabilities. As a consequence of his observation, Feuerstein proposed an extension of Piaget's S-O-R model. Between the stimulus and the learner and the response and the learner,

> Feuerstein adopted the belief that learning is centered in the active mental engagement of the learner.

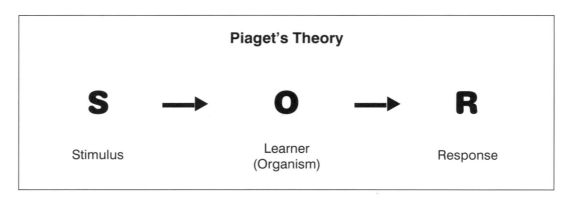

Piaget's Theory

S → O → R

Stimulus   Learner
(Organism)   Response

IRI/SkyLight Training and Publishing, Inc.

Feuerstein added the mediator. This mediator is a person who captures the many stimuli which bombard a learner every day, strains the stimuli, and helps the child develop his own way of filtering those stimuli which promote learning from those that distract. For Feuerstein, parents are the first mediators. They are assisted by peers, siblings, teachers, counselors, and other helpers who assist the learner in developing his learning propensity.

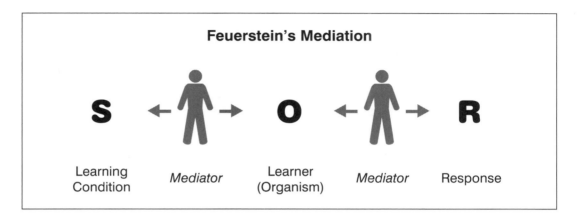

Feuerstein's Mediation

S Mediator O Mediator R

Learning Condition   Mediator   Learner (Organism)   Mediator   Response

To assist the mediation process, Feuerstein developed a curriculum of "content-free" print materials which he called "instruments." In actuality, the content of each instrument is "thinking" itself. Feuerstein wanted this "content-free" approach so that the student would not be blocked by language deficiencies or by a lack of prior knowledge in any specific discipline. Such a lack, he argued, would distract from the cognitive restructuring.

The mediator helps the learner concentrate on the thinking processes he is using to solve the increasingly difficult problems on each instrument. In addition, the mediator, relying on selected open-ended questions and positive feedback, helps the learner identify how he is planning to solve the problem, how he is assessing the process for solving the problem , and what tactics were most successful. Guided by additional open-ended questions from the mediator, the learner identifies the successful process and applies the critical elements to the next, more difficult problem.

Noting how "teacher talk" and mindless seatwork had failed with these children, Feuerstein adapted the inquiry strategies that he had learned as a child psychologist and teacher. These strategies, which he labeled "mediation," became the essential tools for enabling classroom teachers and parents to uncover the cognitive functions necessary for all children, especially children challenged to learn how to learn.

As Feuerstein and his colleagues developed it, mediation is a mutual interaction between the mediator (a parent, teacher, coach, or counselor) and the student. The mediator purposefully directs the interaction toward a specific goal by focusing attention, selecting, framing, interpreting, and

The mediator helps the child develop his own way of filtering those stimuli which promote learning from those that distract.

cuing the student on specific stimuli. Consider again the example of the young student walking home from school. A parent or teacher at his side as he walked through the dilapidated neighborhood could focus his attention on the sights, sounds, and smells. By highlighting what they were experiencing together, the parent or teacher could interpret his experience, establish cause-and-effect relationships, and give meaning to the events. The student's attention could be directed toward different people, and he could make comparisons to other individuals at other places who are similar. Cutting short the student's impulsive and shallow judgments would help him sort through the plethora of experiences systematically. In short, Feuerstein would argue that this caring mediator ensures that the child learns how to learn in a purposeful and complete way. The mediator builds the foundations of cognition, the thinking processes which ensure that the student will learn no matter what means of instruction—direct, indirect, constructive, or collaborative—the child might receive in future schooling. With such mediation the child develops the internal controls that enable him to learn how to learn.

The mediator builds the foundations of cognition, the thinking processes which ensure that the student will learn.

The Criteria for Successful Mediation

Feuerstein developed ten criteria of interaction that are fundamental for skilled mediation. The first three criteria—(1) intentionality and reciprocity, (2) meaning, and (3) transcendence—Feuerstein believes are necessary for successful mediation in any instructional situation. The remaining seven—(4) competence, (5) self-regulation and control of behavior, (6) sharing behavior, (7) individuation, (8) goal-planning, (9) challenge, and (10) self-change—Feuerstein saw as helpful in specific situations. Because they teach children *how* to learn, all of these mediative efforts, he argues, are essential for making high expectations central to every classroom. They are especially important to counter the poor instruction that is provided in classrooms dominated by workbooks, laissez-faire busywork, teacher lectures, and recall tests. The teacher-as-mediator, therefore, is the person who initiates active learning, the mental processing which transforms incidental learners into students grounded in the prerequisites for learning, and leads students to success in each and every content area.

☐ Multiple Intelligences

In the 1980s, Harvard cognitive psychologist Howard Gardner reinforced Feuerstein's position that the intelligence was flexible by advancing the theory of multiple intelligences. Like Feuerstein, Gardner challenged the traditional belief that intelligence was fixed and immutable. Gardner's theory has very powerful implications for instruction in urban classrooms, especially for those many students whose ways of knowing differ from the conventional approaches to learning.

Multiple Intelligences theory brightens the possibilities for what is understood to be a classroom. Instead of thinking of the classroom as a 35' x 35' room where a teacher guides thirty students, all places that are rich learning environments become learning centers. Thus, in Gardner's eyes, a children's museum is not a place limited to field trips—it becomes a classroom rich in learning opportunity; a botanical garden is not simply a place to visit and observe—it is a classroom where children can dig their hands into the dirt. A classroom is not a place to visit for forty minutes of a day—it is an environment rich with materials and tools for making, doing, and expanding many intelligences.

Gardner's theory of multiple intelligences does not occur by happenstance. Gardner supports his theory by choosing rigorous criteria for proposing the existence of his proposed intelligences. Beginning with his definition of intelligence as "the human intellectual competence (which) must entail a set of skills for problem solving—enabling the individual to *resolve genuine problems* or difficulties he or she encounters, and when appropriate to *create an effective product*" (Gardner 1983, 60–61), Gardner expanded his theory and described a multiplicity of intelligences that met his criteria.

Teachers can apply an array of learning opportunities that challenge students well beyond traditional expectations.

For any classroom that contains a child with a special challenge, as easy to include as mild dyslexia, as difficult to include as advanced multiple sclorosis, Gardner's theory rips down the barriers to learning which protect the belief that there is one right way to teach all children. Instead, he provides a strong foundation for the development of classroom environments and instructional strategies that take teachers and students well beyond traditional limits. Freed from perceived constraints on instruction, teachers can apply the theory in an endless array of learning opportunities that challenge students well beyond traditional expectations.

☐ Authentic Learning and Authentic Assessment

One of the largest benefits of Gardner's theory is its allowance for more authentic ways to assess student learning. Conventional assessment, spurred by the use of Scantron marking machines, favors short-answer responses to questions of fact. A student's ability to answer many questions in a short time period becomes the chief measure of her ability to learn. Under the pressures of accountability, teachers mold instruction to fit the short-answer test. Students, knowing the game well, decide how much time and effort they will expend in memorizing facts and figures. Obviously, those with the fastest recall have the least difficulty with rote work; many others, seeing no value to rote work, refuse to play the game.

In the past few years, the focus on student evaluation has switched from short-answer tests and single-score grades to multiple sources of information about what a student knows and does to demonstrate learning, performance standards, and the alignment of classroom instruction with district, state, and national standards. In almost every content field, national commissions work on defining the content and process standards for that discipline. In other areas such as staff development, national associations lead the way in defining standards for that area. Most recently, recognition has begun to be given to the teacher's role in assessing students in multiple ways.

When assessment goes beyond the limits of the #2 pencil standardized test, multiple views emerge regarding what a student knows and is able to do. Thus, in writing, teachers return to assessing how well the student actually prepares a persuasive or an expository essay. The standardized test may show what the student knows about grammar usage, but it is in writing an authentic essay that the student shows how well he can use grammar. In social studies, the short-answer test may show the student's knowledge of the facts in the course; the completion of a service project or the application of key course ideas in a debate show her ability to use the knowledge. By forming standards and criteria for success and by using new tools that challenge the multiple intelligences in a classroom, the teacher can assess both the knowledge and the student's ability to use the knowledge in meaningful ways. When students learn by using knowledge, they are learning by "authentic means"; when the teachers use the standards, the criteria, and the tools to assess that authentic learning, they are performing "authentic assessment."

By its very nature, authentic assessment creates higher expectations than does the simple short-answer test that allows students to escape the responsibility of significant learning. In the high-expectations classroom where students know from day-to-day experience that there is no hiding from the teacher's adherence to high-engagement learning tasks, they know they are accountable to high standards to demonstrate what they know and can do.

Authentic assessment creates higher expectations than does the simple short-answer test.

CHAPTER 2

Intentionality and Reciprocity

One writes out of one thing only—one's own experience. Everything depends on how relentlessly one forces from this experience the last drop, sweet or bitter, it can possibly give. This is the only real concern of the artist, to recreate out of the disorder of life that order which is art.

—James Baldwin
"Notes of a Native Son" (1955)

In our modern, high-tech society, we are all bombarded with stimuli. Events occur rapidly and forcefully; TV ads deliver pictures at a super-fast rate with high volume sound; fast-food signs flash ads for new, quicker meals; and school curricula are jam-packed with facts and details that teachers must cover at an ever-quickening pace.

More than ever, it is important for children to have mediators who can instill the ability to filter out stimuli that distract them from learning and prevent them from making important distinctions among stimuli. If the children lack impulse control, or if they have physical, mental, or emotional challenges that limit their ability to process information with precision and accuracy, they need a system for processing information in an orderly way.

❑ Purpose and Vigilance

In the early stages of every mediation, the caring mediator isolates and interprets the various stimuli and presents the filtered stimuli in a way that encourages the student to respond positively. This act of purposeful mediation is called *intentionality*.

The mediator's work at intentionality, as a filter of concrete experiences, is much like a medical doctor's putting a slide in the microscope and highlighting selected tissue with a colored dye. The doctor does this to point out more easily what he wants other staff to look at. Because the dye makes the special tissue stand out, the others more easily focus on what the doctor has targeted for them. As soon as they focus their attention on the examination of the colored tissue, they are aroused, Feuerstein would say, "to a state of vigilance." This responsive state of vigilance is called *reciprocity*.

The teacher-mediator is concerned about the quality of interaction.

Whether helping a student learn how to compare two objects, complete a mathematics problem, or memorize science vocabulary, the teacher-mediator is concerned about the *quality* of interaction. He begins by helping the student filter out distracting and inappropriate information. If the student's feelings of inadequacy arise as excuses, the teacher-mediator keeps her on track by use of encouragement ("You can do it, I know you can"). If the student is distracted by an overabundance of factual information, the mediator microscopes the key points with cuing ("I want you to start here") and focusing ("Look right here at these two examples"). In large classrooms, the teacher-mediator targets those students who are especially resistive. He does not allow hiding. His tone is firm, respectful, and direct. As students perform the assigned task, he recognizes their success with warm, enthusiastic, and specific feedback: "Good for you! I knew that you could find at least five items for comparing the characters in the story—you found seven! Bravissimo!"

There is nothing wishy-washy about the intention to secure the student's responses. The skilled mediator may go so far as to force eye contact from the student: "Look at me. Read my lips. Follow my finger as it points the way. Your tiredness and your interest in doing something else do not count at this moment. Focus on what I am showing you. Stay with me."

IRI/SkyLight Training and Publishing, Inc.

Before they can have success with intentionality, many mediator candidates must first unlearn the laissez-faire, "be sweet" and "oh, he's so cute!" models on which they have built a lifetime of low-quality interaction with students: "Don't push. Don't embarass. Don't confront. Don't persist with your high expectations for change by the student. Let him construct his own meaning."

Feuerstein teaches the opposite. He knows from his own experience as a survivor of the Holocaust how resilient students are. He also knows that student reciprocity is not enriched when the adult rescues the student from responsibility for learning. He also knows from his work with the children of the Holocaust and with troubled youth from all over the world that unless the parent or teacher expects these youngsters to change how they think and behave, unless the mediator persists in demanding the changes, most students will form low expectations for themselves and stay trapped in the inability to learn.

> **Unless the mediator persists in demanding the changes, most students will form low expectations for themselves.**

Feuerstein also differentiates mediation with respect and care from mean, verbal abuse. Any observer of his intentional mediation with young people will see the bond of caring that he creates. He is firm and pressing while being gentle. One observer called him a pied piper whose interactions with children attracted them to him like magic. The magic he uses starts with his willful insistence that they not engage in escapist behaviors, some as extreme as a child hiding her face behind her hands, a child climbing under a table, or a child burying his head in his arms or clasping his ears. His soft but firm voice urges, empathizes, encourages, and commands; it never whines or begs. And when he notices the first movement that shows his voice is getting through, he applauds, he reaffirms, he whispers his delight, and he strengthens the connection until he has full, willful attention from the child. "Bravo!" is his favorite salute to success.

■ Mediational Strategies that Promote Intentionality

Intentionality suggests purposeful direction. The mediator has two levels of intention when she begins an interaction. First, she wants to engage the student in the lesson or task at hand. She recognizes and strategizes to overcome the student's natural resistances and distractions. She builds on the student's interests and needs.

In addition to the verbal interactions mentioned, the intentional mediator uses visual signs and verbal statements that tell the students the direction she proposes.

Mediational Strategies that Promote Intentionality

- Posted goals and objectives for a lesson

- posted agenda with expected tasks

- posted criteria for assessing student performance

- verbal review and clarification of terms used for goals, agenda, and criteria at the start of a lesson

- verbal questions which ask students to connect tasks in progress with goals and criteria

- map of yearly goals posted in classroom in a sequence

- stories and examples of questions to examine the value and rationale of a lesson or task.

■ Mediational Strategies that Promote Reciprocity

Four major elements invite students to engage in the lesson: checking prior knowledge, task structure, metacognitive reflection, and bridging.

Feuerstein's insistence on respect-building and interaction does not absolve the mediator from amassing a repertoire of inviting strategies that facilitate student reciprocity, especially with resistant or challenged students. These are the nets that the mediator used to snare students and draw them into the learning act. Beyond drawing students into the lesson, the mediating teacher will want the students to go beyond the specifics of the lesson and make more generalized connections. The immediate intention may ask students to learn how to add whole numbers or to name the state capitals. An intention which goes beyond the use of a skill or the recall of a fact may ask students to explain why the information or skill is important, to identify uses or even to make a use or demonstrate an application. These are the transcendent goals that connect the details of learning with the principles of knowing, understanding, and using knowledge.

Obviously, the mediation of intentionality and reciprocity is needed throughout a lesson or unit. As the mediator works through the lesson, she returns time and again to the task of pulling her students, physically and mentally, into what she is teaching. The more her intentionality enables students to engage and reengage themselves in the learning task, the richer the result.

In addition to using mediational strategies, the mediator must weave intentionality and reciprocity through each lesson's design. High quality design will contain four major elements that invite students to engage in the lesson: checking prior knowledge, task structure, metacognitive reflection, and bridging.

Mediational Strategies that Promote Reciprocity

- Using printed words, symbols, and pictures drawn in color on newsprint or blackboard to reinforce lesson objectives, instructions, or rubrics

- designing tasks that move students from concrete manipulatives to abstract symbols

- using a variety of instructional materials at different reading levels to accommodate individual reading readiness

- standing in a single place while addressing the class to lower distraction for students with low focus tolerance

- using graphic organizers such as sequence charts or mind maps to help students see relationships

- teaching vocabulary before starting a lesson

- shortening length of tasks

- visually checking for understanding with hand signals

- honoring all answers to questions by noting what part of the answer was correct and asking other students to add to the correct part

- using the "wraparound" with the pass rule to structure responses to questions

- asking a question before telling a student's name

- daily use of "Today I learned . . ." wraparounds

- starting each class period with a pair review

- using the bulletin board for a connection map

- using a buddy system so that each challenged child has a speciifc partner but isn't singled out

- allowing students to substitute a tape-recorded answer

- providing special materials such as lapboard, felt pens, taped paper, page holders, and turners to assist physically-challenged students.

■ Checking Prior Knowledge

A strong lesson begins with a check of what the students already know about the topic. This provides a context as well as a motivating connection to past learning. In many lessons, there is neither context nor linkage to the student's past knowledge. The teacher not adept at using intentional strategies may introduce a new set of words or a new semantic technique. She makes no attempt to link words found in one chapter to their occurrence in other chapters. These practices reinforce learning as an incidental, isolated, or episodic series of words or events.

Isolated or Incidental Learning

Chapter 1		Chapter 2		Chapter 3
prefixes		suffixes		homonyms

When those urban students who have dispositions to impulsive and episodic learning are reinforced by disconnected and episodic instruction, the results are doubly damaging. The students miss the material and find no way to make sense of how to learn. However, when the teacher mediates these students for intentionality by using a prior knowledge check to start the construction of connections, the teacher not only learns what students may know—she also learns how well the students see a topic's relationship to previous topics. For instance, do the students see how prefixes and suffixes are both important to changing a word's use? If this is noted, it prepares the mediator to point out the connection and use examples from the previous lesson on prefixes to explain suffixes in the new lesson. As the teacher helps provide these connections, the episodic students' discovery of the relationship leads to their increased interest.

By checking prior knowledge, the teacher builds a bridge for the students.

By checking prior knowledge, the teacher builds a bridge for the students and mediates their understanding of the relationships between new ideas and past experience, as well as between intentionality and reciprocity. The teacher is strengthening the students' knowledge of how to learn. Having clarified their existing knowledge of the subject, the teacher has invited the students into a task that will expand the universe of knowing.

The best known tool for checking prior knowledge is Donna Ogle's easy-to-use KWL chart. Using a newsprint chart or blackboard, the teacher outlines the chart:

Topic

K What We **K**now	**W** What We **W**ant to Know	**L** What We **L**earned

IRI/SkyLight Training and Publishing, Inc.

Small groups or the entire class together work to fill in the first column about the topic. When all ideas known to the class are listed, the students generate questions about the topic. At the lesson's conclusion, they complete the final column, with the techer making explicit those connections that the students miss.

☐ Structuring the Task

Because the curricula in many American schools are badly disjointed, teachers routinely say, "It's ten a.m., time for spelling," then at 10:30 a.m. they announce "It's time for mathematics," and so on. One piece is piled atop another, and students who are already episodic are lost in the swirl of the day's events.

Once the mediating teacher has checked prior knowledge, she helps students by following a careful lesson design. Madeline Hunter called the process of task structuring "the making of a string of pearls." She decried the practice of "throwing eggs against the wall" which she observed so many "episodic" teachers doing.

Hunter's design elements provide one helpful list of what teachers can do to structure a learning task. Feuerstein would see these as elements that a teacher might include to invite greater reciprocity:

1. Anticipatory Set
2. Stating the Objective
3. Checking for Understanding
4. Modeling
5. Guiding Practice
6. Giving Independent Practice
7. Closure

For episodic learners, the "set" provides a content fit ("Where does this new lesson fit with what we are learning in this course?").

Checking for understanding is the most important "connection-making" tool the teacher has.

Obviously, checking for understanding, much like road signs along a highway, is the most important "connection-making" tool the teacher has. It provides insurance that students focus on the lesson's objective, staying "on target." As the lesson proceeds, misunderstandings point to the need for explicit "connection making" to ensure that students will arrive at the trip's end as stated in the objective.

In addition to Hunter's lesson design, there are others which use different elements or describe the ingredients with different words. What Hunter contributed was the notion of design as a way to help episodic learners move through new content in an orderly, well-paced fashion.

❑ Looking Back and Reflecting

At the conclusion of a well-structured lesson, time needs to be allotted for episodic learners to reflect on what they have learned and how they have learned. The reflection will start with a strategic review of the content learned in the lesson. It may also call for an assessment of how the students learned and the applications they can make. In essence, this review forces the making of key connections so that students not only see the immediate relationships but also learn how to establish the connections themselves.

❑ Bridging Forward

This establishment of connections in the learning process is furthured in a lesson design under the heading *bridging forward*. The behaviorists' notion of transfer (S–R) says "it doesn't happen." The mediator's notion is that transfer does occur when it is "shepherded" (Fogarty, Perkins, & Barell 1992). A "good shepherd" is one that takes time to structure the purposeful transfer of learning. This occurs when the mediator bridges key lesson concepts into other content areas to be studied or into appropriate life situations.

Note in the following sample lesson how the design includes the four elements described:

- Checking Prior Knowledge
- Structuring the Task
- Looking Back and Reflecting
- Bridging Forward

MIDDLE SCHOOL LESSON

Geography

Problem
How identify geographic regions

Focus Intelligence
Verbal/Linguistic

Supporting Intelligence
Visual/Spatial

■ CHECKING PRIOR KNOWLEDGE

Invite one student from the class to locate on a map or globe: *(a)* Africa, *(b)* Tanzania, *(c)* Mt. Kilimanjaro, *(d)* the Serengeti Plain, *(e)* the Ngorongoro Crater. On newsprint, blackboard, or overhead, show this chart. How can we find the differences among these geographic regions?

	Plain	Mountain	Crater
Know			

Ask the students to volunteer what they know about each word. Fill in the responses. When there are no more responses, draw a dotted line across. Next, identify the geographic areas and an explanation of the three terms: plain, mountain, crater. Let the students know that by the end of this lesson, each will *(a)* know three distinguishing features of a geographic region (plain, mountain, crater), *(b)* how these features are found in one region (Tanzania), and *(c)* how to create an imaginary country with three similar features on another continent.

■ STRUCTURING THE TASKS

Divide the class into heterogeneous base groups of three each. Assign roles (Mapmaker, Scribe, Materials Manager) and provide materials (newsprint, markers, print, or visual materials regarding Tanzania, plains, craters, and mountains) and three questions for each group member to answer about the assigned geographic features.

Mt. Kilimanjaro

Serengeti Plain

Ngorongoro Crater

1. What is the Serengeti Plain? Ngorongoro Crater? Mt. Kilimanjaro?

2. In what ways is it a plain? crater? mountain?

3. How is it a unique place? (i.e., how is the Serengeti Plain different from other plains on this continent or in other parts of the world?)

After each student in a group has answered the three questions (allow thirty minutes), each student will group with two others with the same topic. Allow twenty minutes to share answers and agree on a common answer before returning to the base group. Back in the base group, each will share the questions-responses (fifteen minutes) followed by the outlining of Tanzania on newsprint and by entering pictures or symbols to depict the principal traits of the region. Every member of the group needs to be prepared to explain the picture or symbol selection.

Identify three different mapmakers to describe their group selections (five minutes). Ask the other students to listen for areas of agreement. Discuss these briefly before checking for understanding (five minutes). Check for understanding by asking students at random to explain a term. Ask for thumbs-up (agree) or -down (disagree) votes. Where there is disagreement, ask others to describe their understanding until there is agreement with each definition.

Write the "official" definition of each term on the board or overhead. Instruct each group to select a continent (excluding Antarctica). (You can use a box for a random draw.) The group is to use what it knows about each region's common characteristics to create a country on that continent with the features and characteristics learned in the lesson. Show a sample you have made and point out how each group should label regions and characteristics. Use newsprint for one-dimensional maps or provide materials for a two-dimensional diorama (50–90 minutes).

■ LOOKING BACK

After the groups post the complete products and view each others' work, conduct an all-class discussion.

1. What have the students learned about each of Tanzania's three regions?
2. What have they learned about the general terms "plain," "mountain," and "crater"?
3. If they were to go to the Moon, how would they identify plains, craters, and mountains there?
4. When identifying the similarities and differences of regions, what thinking processes would they use?

■ BRIDGING FORWARD

For student journal entries, select one or more of these tasks:

1. You find yourself lost on what you recognize as a plain. How do you know it is a plain? Tell what resources of the plain will help you survive and why?
2. Select another country with at least three different geographic regions. Explain how you will distinguish each region.

In addition to the four elements, the teacher can enrich a lesson design with additional elements that facilitate learning and understanding:

1. **A problem-centered focus.** Problem-centered lessons sit on a continuum from well-defined to ill-defined. Well-defined problems such as "determine how long it took a train to cover the 236 miles between stations A and B if it traveled the distance at 92 m.p.h." are close-ended with set answers. Ill-defined problems are those such as "investigate the possible causes of this accident. . . ." By structuring a lesson in a problem format, the mediator sets up learning as a process of inquiry, as opposed to rote coverage of information. The mediative teacher presents the problem visually on the board, checks for vocabulary understanding, and asks the students to predict the lesson content. She will then connect the problem to the standard by which she will evaluate their performance. Again, she will write the standard and clarify vocabulary for the students.

2. **Engaging tasks.** After inviting students into a lesson with the check for prior knowledge, the mediator is ready with an engaging and challenging task (such as mapmaking in the Geography lesson) that will deepen their understanding or extend their skills. To heighten active engagement, collaborative investigations that promote sharing behavior (see Chapter 7) will in turn promote student reciprocity. Highest on the list of engaging tools, graphic organizers invite student mental engagement (Lyman & McTighe 1988).

   Each graphic organizer amplifies intention. The mediator selects the organizer as a tool to help students "see" the structure of their thinking about a topic. For instance, the question web shows students how to ask a sequence of questions which apply in like situations. The web helps them identify characteristics of a person, place, event, or concept. When used in a cooperative task, the visual organizer may help students engage print content in a way that promotes comprehension. They can see readily how pieces of information connect one to the other in the form of a thinking pattern that promotes complex thinking.

The mediator selects the organizer as a tool to help students "see" the structure of their thinking.

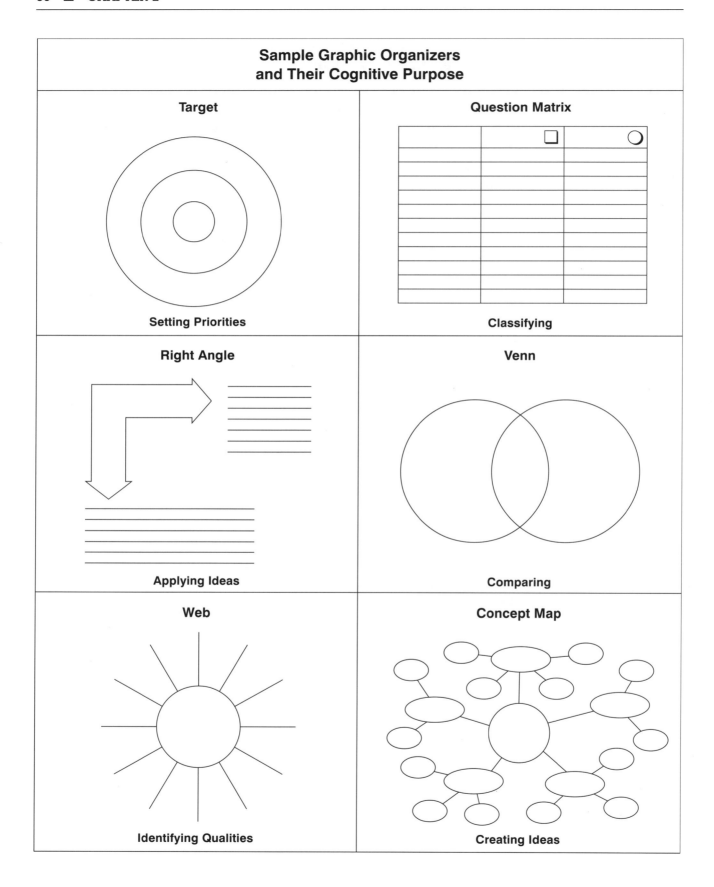

Sample Graphic Organizers and Their Cognitive Purpose

Target

Setting Priorities

Question Matrix

Classifying

Right Angle

Applying Ideas

Venn

Comparing

Web

Identifying Qualities

Concept Map

Creating Ideas

IRI/SkyLight Training and Publishing, Inc.

3. **Project-centered lessons and units.** Projects, especially those carried out in collaborative pairs and trios, are a third tool for challenging students to high mental engagement. Notice how the design in this project ends a unit on "Insects" by elevating the content (insects) with a project to transform the information learned into a thought-provoking experience.

Create a Creature

	A	B	C	D	E	F
	Body Symmetry	Segmentation	Form of Locomotion	Sensory Organs	Support Structures	Body Covering
1	bi-lateral	none	none	eyes, ears, & nostrils	bony skeleton	skin-hair
2	radial	2 body segments	2 or 4 walking legs	paired antennae	cartilaginous skeleton	scales
3	bi-lateral	3 body segments	legs & wings	compound eye & antennae	exoskeleton	skin-hair
4	bi-lateral	multiple segments	6 or 8 legs	tentacles	soft bodied	feathers
5	radial	2 body segments	fins	eyes, ears, & nostrils	shell hinged	scales
6	bi-lateral	none	multiple walking legs	compound eye & antennae	shell carried	skin-hair

Courtesy of Bob Kapheim, York High School, Elmhurst, IL

When a total lesson includes all of these engaging elements in a design that invites students to repond to the curriculum, the teacher can more easily focus on mediating the other interactions that heighten student involvement and result in increased achievement. Note how all the elements mark the design of the following "problem-based" lessons.

MIDDLE SCHOOL LESSON

Social Studies/ Ecology

Problem
How to understand the ways an ecosystem influences the world we live in.

Focus Intelligence
Visual/Spatial.

Supporting Intelligences
Interpersonal and Verbal/ Linguistic.

■ CHECKING PRIOR KNOWLEDGE

1. Invite students to identify the nations or regions from which their families came to the United States. Make a 3" x 8" sign for each student to wear.

2. Ask the students, each wearing one sign, to assemble under one of these signs hung in the room: (a) North America, (b) South America, (c) Central America, (d) Europe, (e) Asia, (f) Africa, (g) Australia. Read the signs to the class and use choral-response to teach pronunciation.

3. Tell the students they are going to learn some ways the environment (explain the word) influences how people in these places live. Show a chart with an example to illustrate how weather impacts natural materials and how natural materials are used to protect against weather. You may want to select three to seven words to teach new vocabulary in the lesson context.

■ STRUCTURING THE TASK

1. Using pictures on a bulletin board or a slide show, show examples of housing from many cultures. Be sure to include samples from students in the class. Here are some starters:

    a. Native American/First Nation

    b. Inuit

    c. Mexican-Indian

    d. Mexico City

    e. East Africa-Masai Herders

    f. Virgin Islands

    g. England

    h. South Pacific Island.

2. Ask the students to explain how and why they think the shelters were so different. How and why are the shelters alike?

3. From heterogeneous groups of three, give each group the materials they'll need to research, sketch, and build a model house from a culture different

from their own. After the model is made, the students will *(a)* label the feature shared with their current homes and *(b)* prepare to explain how the environmental conditions influenced the special features (e.g., the igloo derived from cold weather, ice).

4. Display the finished products for all to see.

■ LOOKING BACK

1. Ask each group to share what it has learned about the influence of environment on the culture studied. Use the completed works to illustrate.

2. Construct a large matrix to display on the bulletin board. Across the top, list the cultures studied in this lesson.

Culture ▶					
House Shape					
Number of Rooms					
Raw Materials					
Uses					
Special Features					
Weather					

After you demonstrate one example, invite the groups to fill in the chart. (You may have to do the writing, or you may allow sketches on cards to fit each block.)

3. Use a wraparound so that each student in turn can respond to this lead in: "In our study of different houses from different lands, I learned. . . . " ("I pass" is allowed.)

4. Summarize the students' statements.

■ BRIDGING FORWARD

For student journal entries, select one or more of the following tasks:

1. Make a list of how the environment in our town or city has influenced our shelters.

2. Make a sketch that matches the environmental factors (e.g., snow) with the elements (e.g., heater) that are in your house.

Assessing Student Performance

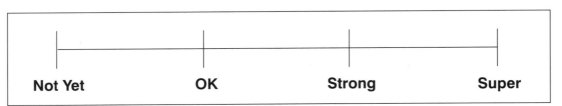

Not Yet   **OK**   **Strong**   **Super**

To what degree can the student (using an example from a nonlocal ecosystem):

1. Explain the connection between key environmental factors and the elements of design and construction in a common shelter?

2. Identify the environmental factors which influence the design and construction of shelters in a selected ecosystem?

Materials

Globe or world map, sign for each continent, pictures of climate conditions in a variety of ecosystems, pictures of homes from 6–12 cultures around the world, art or model-making supplies, and student journals.

Variations

1. Select one ecosystem with unique housing. As a class, build a "life-size" model of the shelter with representative geology and plant life.

2. Select an ecosystem with unique housing and create a representational mural.

IRI/SkyLight Training and Publishing, Inc.

MIDDLE SCHOOL LESSON

Subways and Buses

Problem
How to enjoy a poem.

Focus Intelligence
Verbal/Linguistic.

Supporting Intelligences
All.

■ CHECKING PRIOR KNOWLEDGE

Place the students into heterogeneous groups of three. Ask each group to make a sketch of the perfect subway car or city bus (no limits on comfort!). Call upon groups to show their sketches and explain the design. In the process, record on the board words they use to identify what they know about subways and buses.

■ STRUCTURING THE TASK

1. Provide each group with a poem or song from the collection *Poetry in Motion: 100 Poems from Subways and Buses* (Parchen, Peacock, and Neches, editors; New York: Norton, 1996).

2. Ask each group to study its poem.

   - What does the poem say about the subway or buses? About the city and its people?

   - What feelings does the poem evoke? How does it do so?

   - What do you like or dislike about the poem? Why?

■ LOOKING BACK

Ask each group to read its poem to the class and discuss the responses to the questions. Hold a summary discussion on the elements that promoted enjoyment.

■ BRIDGING FORWARD

Invite each group to compose its own poem about a bus or the subway.

Assessing Student Performance

To what degree:

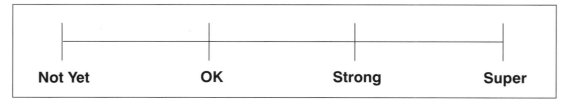

| Not Yet | OK | Strong | Super |

1. Does the poem capture the feeling of urban life?

2. Does the poem use poetic forms?

3. Does the poem deliver a message about urban life?

Materials

Copies of the poems.

Variations

1. Select other examples of urban poems or urban-based short stories.

2. Allow groups to represent buses or the subway in different media such as videos, songs, mobiles, sketches, etc.

IRI/SkyLight Training and Publishing, Inc.

SECONDARY SCHOOL LESSON

Social Studies

Problem
How the Bill of Rights applies to current social problems.

Focus Intelligence
Visual/Spatial, Interpersonal.

Supporting Intelligences
Logical/Mathematical, Interpersonal, Intrapersonal, Visual/Spatial, Verbal/Linguistic.

■ CHECKING PRIOR KNOWLEDGE

Ask each student to complete this agree/disagree chart:

Possible Rights	Agree	Disagree
1. The Bill of Rights says women have a right to vote.		
2. A high school diploma is a right.		
3. Every citizen has a right to own a shotgun.		
4. American citizens have a right to life, liberty, and the pursuit of happiness.		

After students have completed their charts, invite random responses on each statement.

Because many of the items are controversial and you want the students to explore multiple points of view, you are encouraged to mediate student thinking by asking such questions as "Why do you think that?", "What is your evidence or rationale?", etc. Encourage students to defend their points of view with good logic and valid evidence. After each question, show on the overhead the statement from the Bill of Rights which each case statement is related to. Highlight instances from the above discussion that touched on the Bill of Rights.

■ STRUCTURING THE TASK

Explain the purpose of the problem-centered task. Give each group a copy of the Bill of Rights and one of the four case statements. Using the Bill of Rights, each group is to make a ruling on the constitutionality of the case and develop its rationale in a written essay. Rotate the papers so that one other group gives feedback on each team's essay. (You may also want to read and give feedback.) When all feedback is given, conduct an all-class discussion on the disagreements.

■ LOOKING BACK

Instruct each group to examine the steps it took in completing the task. Post these questions as a guide:

1. What steps in problem-solving did you use to connect the case to the Bill of Rights?

2. In your discussions, what were the areas of most agreement? disagreement?

3. How did you resolve the disagreements?

4. How did you montior your own behavior during the "hot" moments of discussion?

5. If you were to do a second case, what changes would you make in your process?

After the group discussions, sample the responses with a classwide discussion.

■ BRIDGING FORWARD

In journals, invite students to write:

1. What they learned about the Bill of Rights.

2. How they might react in the future to a personal challenge that posed a threat to their constitutional rights.

Assessing Student Performance

To what degree can the student:

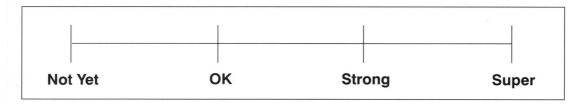

1. Explain why the Bill of Rights is an important document?

2. Identify the rights contained in the Bill of Rights?

3. Describe how the Bill of Rights is used in ruling on the constitutionality of a court case?

Materials

Agree/Disagree charts, copies of the Bill of Rights, and case statements.

Variations

1. Substitute other parts of the Constitution as the tool for judging a problem.

2. Invite students to create "real life" legal cases from their own experiences.

3. Enact a mock trial around a signficant case. Assign student teams as prosecutors, defense, judicial panel, etc.

4. Conclude with a final discussion of the Agree/Disagree Chart.

When using intentionality and reciprocity, the teacher invites students to a learning party. For some students, a single mailed invitation is sufficient. Others need a follow-up phone call or a special "don't forget tonight" re-minder. Some may turn down even the most glamorous invitation. The skilled mediator understands that a single invitation may not work for all and instead makes allowances for the different needs of students with their different "readinesses to learn" by adjusting, repeating, modifying, and repeating the invitation until each student "shows up" at the party.

IRI/SkyLight Training and Publishing, Inc.

Meaning

Don't take another
mouthful before you
have swallowed what is
in your mouth.

—Madagascan proverb

Very often, parents and teachers are faced with the question "Why?" from an inquisitive child; for the insecure parent or the inexperienced teacher, the quick defense is "Because I said so, that's why!" What is missed in such instances, though, is the child's need to understand the purpose, rationale, or compelling "why" that will make clear the task's or activity's significance. Most often, that answer is best found within the values and beliefs of the family's culture. Rather than give a quick "I said so," the parent or teacher helps the child by providing a patient mediation of *meaning*.

◻ The Mediation of Meaning

The mediation of meaning occurs when the parent or teacher connects the child's "wonder" to a value-rich understanding of purpose and significance at both the cognitive and affective levels. At the cognitive level, the mediator communicates important values and beliefs; at the affective level, the mediator transmits enthusiasm for the belief. The child thus receives compelling and energetic explanations to match her compelling questions of why. In this way, the mediator, a significant guide, moves the interaction to a more profound level of mental and emotional engagement than was provided by the mediation of intentionality. In the mediation of intentionality, the mediator broke down the student's resistance and invited her to consider the possibility of learning something of importance: he captured attention and the student agreed to listen. In the mediation of meaning, though, the mediator charges the learning experience with value and energy, inviting the student to understand the compelling "why."

For Feuerstein, the mediation of meaning has special import. Because the value he speaks about is grounded in the student's culture, it is the mediator's task to connect the student to the inherent power of their culture. The mediator can accomplish this by interpreting and explaining at ever-deepening levels of understanding the significance of the student's heritage. In essence, the mediator is the translator, celebrator, and transmitter of cultural heritage, with all of its knowledge, traditions, values, and beliefs, to the next generation.

> In the mediation of meaning, the mediator charges the learning experience with value and energy.

For most youngsters growing up in a family able to mediate its culture's meaning, the parents are the first mediators. For those whose family is destroyed or disabled by poverty, racism, war, or other causes, there is a great chance that the children will miss the mediation that sets the foundation for successful learning, thinking, and problem-solving.

History is replete with examples of cultures destroyed and disabled: in Canada, there was the institutionalization of the First Nations peoples; in America, the creation of slave quarters for the Africans, of reservations for Native Americans, and of prison camps for American citizens of Japanese descent; in Germany, there was the Holocaust; and in Bosnia and Rwanda, we have witnessed ethnic cleansing. In all of these cases, and in the abundant number of cases like them, many children who survived did so with their cultural identity severely impaired or irretrievably lost.

◻ Combatting the Destruction of Culture

First Nations advocate Lorna Williams was a child who survived in the face of grave difficulties. Taken from her family and sent to boarding school by the Canadian government, Lorna was taught to forget her family and her heritage. Achievement tests administered by the Provincial Government indicated that she and forty-five of the forty-seven young people from her village were "retarded." Hoping to eradicate beliefs they labeled as "primitive," her teachers ridiculed her family, debunked her customs and beliefs, raised self-doubt about her abilities to learn, and frightened her into giving up "the old ways." The school's low expectations and destructive instruction practices almost worked. It was not long before the traditional ways of knowing and acting, which taught her how and why to control her behavior, show respect for her elders, and learn from the examples of the natural world, were beginning to appear stupid, foolish, and superstitious.

Confused, Lorna returned home for summer vacation. Happily, a relative, strong in her own cultural beliefs, intervened. Through story, song, and parental talk, her aunt returned Lorna to the roots of her culture and restored her beliefs in herself, in her people, and in their traditions. From that experience, and other experiences that Feuerstein would label as the true mediation of meaning in her life, Lorna grew as a student, vowing that she too would find ways to help her peers maintain the integrity of their culture. Today, Lorna leads the First Nations Project for the Vancouver Public Schools, consults with school districts across the United States and Canada, and has initiated her doctoral study at Harvard.

Lorna's commitment to finding the best ways to help the children of the First Nations survive in the modern world, and yet retain their traditional ways of "making sense," brought her to the work of Reuven Feuerstein. She quickly connected his teachings about "meaning" to her own travails and triumphs. More importantly, she recognized that his approach, the mediation of learning within the cultural context, would help larger numbers of children than would the tutorial approach her aunt had used to help her recover from what the government school had tried to force upon her.

The assimilation of meaning begins with what we learn as children. What a child learns is rooted in the culture and values of the family. If the culture and the values of a family are systematically discounted, as in Lorna's case, or destroyed, as in the case of the Holocaust children, or if the family is uprooted from its environment, as in the case of the Africans brought to America, it becomes extremely difficult for the child to extract meaning from the world around. Without the mediation that starts in the family, the child is left to learn in episodic and impulsive fits and starts.

Feuerstein's successful work with the children of the Holocaust demonstrated that there is hope for young learners approaching adolescence with cognitive levels lower than their ability; Lorna's work with the First Nations' children and similar projects around the world reinforces the message. The mediation of meaning is a necessary and powerful learning tool for all children who have experienced damage to their cultural roots.

The mediation of meaning is a necessary and powerful learning tool for all children.

■ Strategies for the Mediation of Meaning

In the classroom, a teacher can mediate meaning in a variety of simple but powerful ways. This mediation can start with an enthusiastic explanation of the value of the subjects or topics that the curriculum introduces. The teacher's facial expressions, hand motions, and tone of voice communicate in subtle ways how the topics have value not only in the classroom but in applications to life as well. In addition, the explanation of reasons for classroom rules, modeling behavior for appropriate interactions with other students, and discussions of classroom procedures add to the mediation of meaning. When the teacher makes explicit the strategies, skills, and procedures needed for a learning task (such as solving a mathematics problem or writing an expository essay) and asks questions that engage the students in examining the "why" of such procedures, meaning is successfully mediated. When the teacher illuminates the curriculum to examine the underlying significance of themes and issues as they relate to the values and beliefs of the students, she mediates meaning at the deepest level.

The daily curriculum provides many opportunities for mediating meaning with the students. With curricula typically being overloaded, the meaning-mediating teacher does not want to add additional material for students to cover superficially. The concept of "less is more" comes into play here. For the mediation of meaning, it is helpful to students if the teacher judiciously and selectively abandons material that is removed from student interests and focuses instead on material that is relevant to the students in each class. By building on their relevant prior knowledge or familiarity with each topic, such material will help the students construct deeper understanding of the content they are being presented with.

The construction of meaning is what goes on in the head of a student. It is the mediator's job to make curriculum and instruction decisions that help each student make sense of daily lessons. The more the student is responsible for actual sense-making, the deeper will be the student's understanding; the more the teacher has to tell the student what sense to make of a lesson or of lesson material, the less the student will develop. The mediator, the person who intervenes between the student and the new material, plays a critical role in active facilitation of the sense-making processes.

> Mediation can start with an enthusiastic explanation of the value of the subjects that the curriculum introduces.

Links with Prior Knowledge

A variety of strategies lend themselves to the mediateion of meaning. As introduced earlier (cf. chapter 2) sense-making begins with the classroom teacher's linkage of the students' prior knowledge or familiarity with a new topic or concept. Donna Ogle devised the KWL strategy as a visual, easy-to-use prior knowledge check. After asking the class to list all that they think they know (K) on a topic, she prompts them to list what they think they want (W) to know; at the end of the unit, she will help the students check back on what they learned (L) as a review and closure. For instance, here is a sample KWL chart completed by a fifth-grade class for the unit covering ancient Egypt.

Topic		
K What We **K**now	**W** What We **W**ant to Know	**L** What We **L**earned
the Pyramids the Sphinx King Tut Moses and the Red Sea they liked cats the desert	Why did they embalm the pharoahs? Where is modern Egypt? How did they build their monuments? Why did they build them?	the religion of the Egyptians their modern government how archeology is handled in Egypt Egypt's place in the Middle East

The KWL format has several advantages as a learning tool. First, it helps students recall knowledge about a topic that they have studied in other classes, seen videos of on TV, or read about in books. This list helps the teacher know what the students already know so as not to spend time reworking the curriculum and prompting moans of "We did that already!" It also gives her quick insight into what they do not know on the topic. Finally, it gives a framework for checking the depth of their understanding and for evaluating what specific parts of the planned unit need amendment or deletion.

The most important benefit of this strategy, however, is its provision for the student of a solid foundation on which he can build new knowledge. This foundation provides a readily understandable rationale for studying the topic. It also creates the bridges that enable the student to extend or to deepen knowledge through writing, discussion, and other modes of expression that help with the elaboration processes.

When students are challenged to start with what they know, their level of interest rises.

When students are challenged to start with what they already know on a topic, their level of interest rises (teacher educator Madeline Hunter ranked interest as one of the pre-eminent motivational factors). As students call up what they have learned, they are asked to think about what else they would like to learn on the topic. Although this is a difficult challenge for students who have always let the teacher do all the talking, cuing and delving strategies soon bring them around. Once they begin posing questions that they know will get answered, students' willingness to ask questions on the topic increases as the lesson, project, or unit unfolds.

Explicit Thinking across the Curricula

The second strategy that helps students make sense of subjects in the curriculum is their learning how to use higher-order thinking skills. The literature on metacognition—that is, thinking about thinking—reveals the importance of this strategy in improving student achievement. This particular kind of questioning speeds the process of student inquiry and leads to student readiness to read and listen more critically.

Thinking about Thinking

The first way to help students learn how to think more skillfully is to make explicit the key "thinking processes" implicit in most curricula. For instance, "prediction" is a key reading skill that is introduced in the third grade. Most standardized tests show how well students can use this skill. A few students are natural predictors. Most others can benefit from direct instruction that helps them develop the skill and use it to improve their reading comprehension and test scores. The lesson on the following pages provides a model to help all students develop this thinking ability.

MIDDLE SCHOOL LESSON

Learning about Predictions

Problem
To improve the skill of predicting.

Focus Intelligence
Verbal/Linguistic

Supporting Intelligence
Logical/Mathematical

■ BACKGROUND

One of the conclusions that we have reached about skillful thinkers is that they are risktakers who use data to make sound predictions. The better they are as thoughtful students of data, the more successful they are as predictors. In essence, they do not need to take wild guesses; they take calculated risks based on careful study. Their bets are usually safe bets. Studies also show that the skill to make predictions in reading correlates strongly with the skill to make predictions in critical thinking.

■ CHECKING FOR PRIOR KNOWLEDGE

1. Invite one student to the front of the classroom. Show a coin and predict whether it will come up heads or tails.

2. Have the student flip the coin and tell you whether you were correct or not. Ask the class to guess how many times out of a hundred flips it will come up heads? out of a thousand flips?

■ STRUCTURING THE TASK

1. Using the board or overhead, provide the students with this information:

   A definition of "prediction": anticipating what will occur with a high degree of success (at least eighty percent of the time).

   Identify when prediction is important: in reading fiction, in scientific experiments, in detective work, in a surgical operation, and in math problem-solving.

2. Distribute copies of the short story "The Dinner Party." Prefold the sheets on the lines.

3. Post the BET strategy and explain why it is helpful for this lesson:

   B ase on facts.

   E xamine clues for probability and possibility.

   T ender your bet and make a guess.

4. Invite the students to silently read the first segment. When they are ready, tell them to use BET to predict what will happen next. Elicit responses by identifying the facts, discussing the clues, and making solid guesses.

5. Continue through each segment.

■ LOOKING BACK

Invite students to answer the following:

1. Explain BET in your own words.

2. What are some times that you might use BET (in and out of school)? Explain and clarify.

3. How is this method of reading different from what you ordinarily have done?

4. What would happen if you were to use BET in preparing for your next major test?

5. What are the advantages and disadvantages to using BET? (Make a chart.)

■ BRIDGING FORWARD

1. Instruct the students to write a telegram to the President or a Member of Congress. In the telegram, make a prediction, based on known facts, of what will happen if a specific policy is followed, OR . . .

2. Write a telegram to the student government and make a prediction what will happen if . . . . Collect the telegrams and read samples.

Variations

1. For K–3 use of BET, draw for this list of books or stories that help with prediction:

Aardema, Verna. *Who's in Rabbit's House? A Masai Tale*. Retold by Verna Aardema, illustrated by Leo Dillon and Diane Dillon. Dial Press, 1977.

Asbjornsen, P. C., and J. E. Moe. *The Three Billy Goats Gruff*. Illustrated by Marcia Brown, Harcourt Brace Jovanovich, 1957.

Blackburn, Carol, and Libby Handy. *The Thing from Somewhere*. Ashton Scholastic, 1975.

Brandenberg, Franz. *Nice New Neighbors*. Illustrated by Aliki. Greenwillow, 1977.

Brown, Margaret Wise. *Where Have You Been?* Scholastic-TAB Publications Ltd.

Charlip, Remy. *Fortunately*. Four Winds, 1964.

Emberley, Ed. *Wing on a Flea*. Little, Brown, 1961.

Farber, Norma. *As I Was Crossing Boston Common*. E. P. Dutton and Company, Inc., 1973.

Gag, Wanda. *Millions of Cats*. Coward-McCann, 1928.

Hogrogian, Nonny. *One Fine Day*. Macmillan, 1971.

Hutchins, Pat. *Don't Forget the Bacon*. Greenwillow, 1976.

Mosel, Arlene. *Tikki Tikki Tembo*. Holt, Rinehart, and Winston, CBC Inc., 1968.

Shulevitz, Uri. *One Monday Morning*. Scribner's, 1967.

Yashima, Taro. *Umbrella*. Viking, 1958.

2. Select other short stories for the practice of predicting with older students.

Collier, Eugenia. "Marigolds."

Connell, Richard. "The Most Dangerous Game."

McCullers, Carson. "Like That."

Plath, Sylvia. "Imitation."

Poe, E. A. "The Pit and the Pendulum."

Poe, E. A. "The Cask of Amontillado."

THE DINNER PARTY
By Mona Gardner

The country is India. A colonial official and his wife are giving a large dinner party. They are seated with their guests—army officers, government attachés and their wives, and a visiting American naturalist—in their spacious dining room, which has a bare marble floor, open rafters, and wide glass doors opening onto a veranda.

(BET what will happen next. Why do you think so? Find data to support your idea. Read to verify.)

———————————————————————————————————————

A spirited discussion springs up between a young girl who insists that women have outgrown the jumping-on-a-chair-at-the-sight-of-a-mouse era and a colonel who says that they haven't.

"A woman's unfailing reaction in any crisis," the colonel says, "is to scream. And while a man may feel like it, he has that ounce more of nerve control than a woman has. And that last ounce is what counts."

(BET...)

———————————————————————————————————————

The American does not join in the argument but watches the other guests. As he looks, he sees a strange expression come over the face of the hostess. She is staring straight ahead, her muscles contracting slightly. With a slight gesture she summons the native boy standing behind her chair and whispers to him. The boy's eyes widen and he quickly leaves the room.

Of the guests, none except the American notices this or sees the boy place a bowl of milk on the veranda just outside the open doors.

(BET...)

———————————————————————————————————————

The American comes to with a start. In India, milk in a bowl means only one thing—bait for a snake. He realizes there must be a cobra in the room. He looks up at the rafters, the likeliest place, but they are bare. Three corners of the room are empty and in the fourth the servants are waiting to serve the next course. There is only one place left—under the table.

His first impulse is to jump back and warn the others, but he knows the commotion would frighten the cobra into striking. He speaks quickly, the tone of his voice so arresting that it sobers everyone.

"I want to know just what control everyone at this table has. I will count to three hundred—that's five minutes—and not one of you is to move a muscle. Those who move will forfeit fifty rupees. Ready!"

(BET...)

———————————————————————————————————————

The twenty people sit like stone images while he counts. He is saying " . . . two hundred and eighty . . . " when, out of the corner of his eye, he sees the cobra emerge and make for the bowl of milk. Screams ring out as he jumps to slam the veranda doors safely shut.

"You were right, Colonel," the host exclaims. "A man has just shown us an example of perfect control."

"Just a minute," the American says, turning to his hostess. "Mrs. Wynnes, how did you know that cobra was in the room?"

A faint smile lights up the woman's face as she replies, "Because it was crawling across my foot."

Along with the skill of predicting, there are many other embedded "thinking skills" across the curriculum (e.g., classification in biology and chemistry, attribution in social studies and language arts, and summarization throughout the curriculum).

Inquiry

A second way to develop students' thinking about thinking is to use an inquiry approach. Inquiry will focus students' attention on skills needed to master curricular content. For instance, in biology, as students prepare to categorize, they must be prepared to make logical comparisons. Note how the teacher in the following example uses only questions to mediate meaning in the making of comparisons.

TEACHER: Who would like to draw a comparison between page 3, which we shall deal with today, and pages 1 and 2. Yes, Daniella?

DANIELLA: Here, like on pages 1 and 2, we have to write down what is similar and what is different, but this time we are presented with words rather than pictures.

TEACHER: Very true, Daniella. Could you tell us, in a few words, what the pages have in common?

DANIELLA: The kind of exercise, or activity.

TEACHER: Right, they have the activity in common. And in what way are they different? Try to use one word.

DANIELLA: How can I use one word to say that instead of pictures we have words?

TEACHER: Pictures, words, numbers, drawings, and symbols (writes on the blackboard) all have a common use. What is the function of all of these? Please, Mildred.

MILDRED: They tell us something or give us a message.

TEACHER: Very good, Mildred. Every one of these forms of telling us something or giving us a message is called a language or a modality (writes on the board). So how can we sum up our comparison of the pages? Yes, Anita.

ANITA: They have the activity in common, but they differ in modality.

TEACHER: Excellent. Let us now take the first pair of words. What do a church and a factory have in common? Juan.

JUAN: They are both buildings.

TEACHER: Very true. But is the fact that they are buildings their most important and most essential common attribute?

JUAN: Yes, I think it is.

TEACHER: You know, class, near my neighborhood there is a factory that manufactures bricks. It has a big sign that reads: Benedict Brown's Brick Factory. However, all the activity in this factory takes place in a big yard, in the open air, and not even the smallest building is present. Should this not be considered a factory? Roberto?

ROBERTO: Yes, but most factories are in buildings.

TEACHER: This is true, Roberto. But if factories that are not in buildings are also considered factories, then perhaps factories have some other common attribute which is more critical or essential. Yes, Jerry.

JERRY: Perhaps they should be called places where people manufacture things.

TEACHER: Excellent, Jerry. This is indeed a more essential attribute. Except that we cannot relate this attribute to churches also. Let's take a look at the list of words I'm writing on the blackboard: church, factory, school, public library, sports center, youth club, municipal center, hospital—how can we refer to all of these with just one word, one concept? Yes, Maria.

MARIA: I think I know what you mean, but I can't say it.

TEACHER: Well, we can refer to all these things as *organizations* or *institutions*. (Writes on the blackboard.) Now, who can help me by describing how we came to this conclusion? What were the steps in our thinking that made this a successful comparison? Juan?

Helping Students Connect Culture with Academic Work

A third strategy for developing meaning is in classroom strategies that encourage students to connect their own worlds and cultures to their academic work. Tasks and assignments that help students investigate the worlds they know best, as a means to achieving academic goals in the basic subject areas, are powerful motivators. In the middle grades, a writing assignment that can help students expand knowledge of their heritage while improving their writing or speaking skills is a meaningful learning tool.

MIDDLE SCHOOL LESSON

Writing—My First Autobiography

Problem
How to help middle school students explain their heritage through writing.

Focus Intelligence
Verbal/Linguistic.

Supporting Intelligences
Intrapersonal, Interpersonal, Visual/Spatial, Bodily/ Kinesthetic.

■ CHECKING FOR PRIOR KNOWLEDGE

1. Sit the students in a circle. Ask each one to think of some way that he or she is special. To cue them, show a chart that lists physical characteristics (height, weight, skin color, eye color), favorite games, family size and members, languages spoken at home, pets, places visited, birthdate, etc. Ask each child in turn to pick one thing and share it with the class.

2. After all have finished, ask them to share ways that members of the class are similar and different. Conclude by indicating that they are going to write a profile all about themselves, called an autobiography.

■ STRUCTURING THE TASK

1. Give each student a set of materials and show them how to fold the construction paper in half. If any student is having difficulty, promote sharing behavior by asking another to help. Punch holes a half inch from the fold, thread the yarn, and tie a bow. Take a photo of each child and have the child glue it to the front.

2. On the front cover, have each student print his/her name. On the remaining seven pages, take ten minutes each day to have the children answer these questions:

   - Who am I?
   - My name is _____
   - I am _____ years old
   - I live at _____ in _____
   - I live with _____
   - At home we speak these languages: _____
   - My favorite things are:

Animal	Toy	Hobby	Sport	TV show
Food	Book	Song	School subject	

   Encourage the students to add reasons for each entry.

3. What do I know about my heritage (ask each student to describe his/her nationality or nationalities)? Where is the nation? What is it noted for? What are the foods, music, and language? If you have only a few nationalities represented, you may ask parents from each to share these answers with the entire class. Or you may want the students to interview their parents before they write their own answers.

4. What do I do well? (Before starting this, have the students brainstorm a class list of possible answers about their talents, likes, etc.)

5. When I grow up, what would I like to be? (Before beginning this segment, tell some of the dreams you had as a child. Ask students to add "Why?" to their responses.)

6. When I am a friend to someone, how do I show it? (Before beginning this segment, share your story or read a story about friends.)

7. What do I like about my community? (Before starting this task, help the class brainstorm ideas. Ask them to draw a picture that illustrates what they like about the community.)

■ LOOKING BACK

Put the students into pairs. Invite each to share his or her autobiography with a peer. The listening partner tells what he or she likes about the life story.

■ BRIDGING FORWARD

Use the content from their responses to teach the next step of composition such as sentence construction or paragraph construction with correct punctuation.

Materials

Construction paper (12" x 18"), yarn, hole puncher, camera, film, felt-tip marker, glue, pencils, and crayons.

Variations

1. Use preprinted questions.

2. Use the content from their responses to make a mini-speech to the class: Who I Am.

Curriculum Materials and Life Experiences

The fourth strategy, the one with the most potential for engaging urban students in the making of meaning, but also the most underused, is the selection of curriculum materials closely connected to their life experiences. If advancement in learning starts with prior knowledge and experience, why don't urban students see more science experiments that relate to urban life?

Why don't math problems deal with items the urban students know about? Why can't they hear of the African American and Hispanic American history-makers who contributed to the growth of the American nation? Most especially, why don't urban students have more chances to study the literature of high-caliber writers who describe the pains and joys of American city life?

The lack of curricular materials that provide examples drawn from urban life is clearly attributable to the prevailing practice of the textbook industry. Urban school districts buy what the textbook publishers produce. To find a high-quality science program that features urban settings or a language arts program that devotes as much space to the poems of Gwendolyn Brooks, Maya Angelou, Langston Hughes, Nikki Giovanni, or Rita Dove as it does to those by Chaucer, John Donne, Lord Byron, or Edgar Allan Poe is extremely difficult. The books that most schools use in their curricula place the urban student at a distinct disadvantage. Most urban students' prior knowledge comes up blank when they start with the moors of England, sea adventures, castles, or characters that wear funny metal suits. On the other hand, when what they are asked to read *begins* with the streets of a city, with characters like the people they see each day, the prior knowledge foundation is there to start the meaning-making process that is central to interest and to learning.

In most cases today, it's up to the individual teacher to select curriculum materials, if the system allows it, that connect urban students more directly to the worlds they already know and experience day-to-day. This means that the teacher will have to adjust science experiments, select literature, and find social studies materials that make the direct connections. With this material in hand, she will need to adapt the lessons and units so that the students meet the same curricular goals, but get there by a different pathway.

☐ Adapting the Standard Curriculum

Consider the three sample lessons that follow, which illustrate different ways of adapting a standard curriculum for the benefit of urban students.

PRIMARY SCHOOL LESSON

Cows and Chickens: A Math Lesson

Problem
How to solve a math problem.

Focus Intelligence
Logical/Mathematical.

Supporting Intelligences
Verbal/Linguistic, Visual/Spatial, and Interpersonal.

■ CHECKING PRIOR KNOWLEDGE

1. Ask the class to tell you what they know about cows and chickens.
2. Sketch each animal as they reply.

■ STRUCTURING THE TASK

1. Write on the board: There are four cows and three chickens. How many feet and tails are there all together?
2. Put students into pairs and give each pair one pencil and one piece of paper. Invite them to agree on one answer to the question. They can do work on the paper to figure out the answer. Invite them to make their notations large enough for others to see from the class circle.
3. Check for understanding of the task.
4. Circulate among the pairs and observe how they work together to solve the problem.

■ LOOKING BACK

1. Assemble the pairs in the class circle. Ask a number of the pairs to share what they did to solve the problem. Ask them to save their answers. Invite all to use their listening skills when they are not speaking.
2. Comment on each strategy with positive feedback.

■ BRIDGING FORWARD

1. Ask random pairs to tell what they learned about problem-solving.
2. Identify the answers.

This primary-grade mathematics task requires only a small change to adapt it to the urban experience. Instead of starting with cows and chickens, which many of the urban students might never have seen, the teacher can substitute familiar objects such as dogs and pigeons. The problem then reads, "There are four dogs and three pigeons. How many feet and tails are there altogether?" and meaning-making is speeded up for the urban child.

It is important not only for students to obtain information, especially when that information has connection to their prior knowledge and experience, but also for students to use that information. The more stimulating and creative the opportunity for use, the more likely it is that students will "make sense" of the raw information. By transforming print information into another medium, the students will have a richer opportunity to develop a second or third intelligence, lock the information into short-term memory, and build a sense of pride in their work. In essence, as Feuerstein points out, the teacher structures a meaningful task. In addition, the task provides multiple opportunities for the teacher-mediator to mediate for meaning as the project unfolds. Note in the sample lesson that follows how the "substance abuse prevention" lesson for middle-grade students is high in urban interest as well as rich with opportunity for mediation work. Note as well that it requires less adaptation for urban students than did "Cows and Chickens."

MIDDLE SCHOOL LESSON

Substance Abuse Prevention

Problem
How to conduct a schoolwide anti-drug campaign.

Focus Intelligence
Visual/Spatial.

Supporting Intelligences
Interpersonal, Naturalistic.

■ CHECKING PRIOR KNOWLEDGE

Ask the class to vote on these questions by raising hands for each "yes":

How many have ever seen a political campaign?

How many have seen the TV ads against drugs?

How many have ever marched in a parade?

■ STRUCTURING THE TASK

1. Brainstorm with the class all the ways it could use to advertise the goal of having a drug-free school (e.g., bumper stickers, TV ads, school parade). Select the best five or six.

2. Divide the class into workteams. Each team will select one of the brainstormed ways to advertise for a drug-free school.

3. Each team will go to work so that everyone has a different job, but everyone contributes. Set a schedule or timeline. Indicate how much class time they can use for planning, working, practicing, etc.

4. As a first task, each team will write out an action plan for your approval. Each plan will describe the team's goal, the benefits, the tasks that need to be completed, the timeline, and the materials needed. (This is a low-budget campaign, so encourage the teams to be creative and cheap!)

5. Help the teams work. When the products are ready, have the entire class discuss the coordination of the campaign. Be sure to involve the principal!

■ LOOKING BACK

Ask the class to respond to these questions:

What did we do well to communicate our message?

What could we improve if we did it again?

What did we learn?

Have the students tabulate the data collection from the other classes. On the basis of the data, ask the class to reevaluate its campaign with the three questions and with a discussion of what they learned *(a)* about designing a campaign for a drug-free school, and *(b)* about teamwork.

The third sample lesson calls for a more complex adaptation. At the secondary level, it is as easy to substitute a quality urban novel or autobiography in the English curriculum as it is to select an important work from Merry Olde England or Puritan America. For instance, instead of studying the trials and tribulations of Hester Prynne in *The Scarlet Letter*, the English teacher in the urban classroom might introduce her students to Bigger in *Black Boy*. To replace Boswell's *Life of Johnson*, the urban teacher might substitute the *Autobiography of Malcolm X*. Better yet, the teacher might pair two novels such as Toni Morrison's *Beloved* and Crane's *Red Badge of Courage* to compare characters against a common theme.

SECONDARY SCHOOL LESSON

Literature: Understanding Malcolm X

Problem
How to understand through literary analysis the attributes of Malcolm X.

Focus Intelligence
Verbal/Linguistic.

Supporting Intelligences
Interpersonal, Intrapersonal, Visual/Spatial.

■ CHECKING PRIOR KNOWLEDGE

After students have read *Malcolm X*, assign groups of three to make a concept map of Malcolm X's character. Let each group take specific scene(s) as the information source. Using what he says, what he does, and what others say about him, they will determine which characteristics or traits are most evident. After each group charts its section, assemble the all-class chart showing what they know about this person.

■ STRUCTURING THE TASK

Begin by creating a class list which best describes those traits of Malcolm X's that led to his death. Brainstorm to generate the list and then keep only those traits that get sixty percent or more of the vote. Next, use the trios (above) to pick the traits that, if changed, might have led to a different ending. Have each group select one of these and identify where in the *Autobiography* it would appear, what Malcolm X or others would say or do to reflect the trait, and how the *Autobiography* would end as a result. Discuss all the variations before asking each trio to create the lines and act out the final scene.

■ LOOKING BACK

Ask each student to make a journal entry describing five things they learned about Malcolm X. Match student pairs and have each student talk for one minute about one learning. Do not repeat. Form a new match of pairs. Give each thirty seconds to share a new learning. Make a third pairing and allow fifteen seconds for each.

■ BRIDGING FORWARD

1. Ask each student to make a journal entry that summarizes what was learned from Malcolm X and that describes the applicability to his life is. Do a wraparound closure; or
2. Ask each student to write a five paragraph essay describing the character of Malcolm X and/or the lessons to be learned from the decisions he made.

IRI/SkyLight Training and Publishing, Inc.

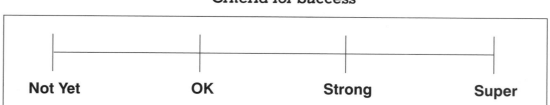

Criteria for Success

|Not Yet|OK|Strong|Super|

1. Identify three to five attributes of the main character and explain why each is unique to this person.
2. Describe the process used for analyzing a literary character.

Materials

A copy of the text of *The Autobiography of Malcolm X* for each student and student journals.

Variations

1. Substitute any short story, drama, novel, biography, or autobiography from the curriculum with a focus on the main character.
2. Show the *Malcolm X* video and assign groups to contrast various elements with the *Autobiography*.
3. Use magazine stories about a current public figure.
4. Use original historical documents and textbook entries about a public figure.
5. Conduct student interviews with local officials, prominent community leaders, family, or friends.
6. Cite supporting characters in a story. Assign one character to a group. Contrast the characters.
7. Do a comparative study of Boswell's *Life of Samuel Johnson* with the *Autobiography*.

Meaning is inherent to every lesson in the curriculum. If curricula or instructional practices leave the impression with students that learning is a piecemeal task or a series of discrete tasks ("Why do we have to use correct grammar in a history paper? Isn't grammar for language arts?"), students need to see meaning in what they are learning. If they are episodic learners already, the damage is double. Therefore, it is doubly important for teachers to double their efforts as they mediate for meaning in the urban classroom with adaptations in lesson design, materials, and units of learning. There are a multitude of other strategies and methods that facilitate the mediation of meaning. These strategies and methods are less important than the mediator's intentionality in making sure that students are in a position to take advantage of understanding the meanings; with this intention, the selection of helpful tools will make the task easier.

Transcendence

Children have never
been very good at listen-
ing to their elders, but
they have never failed to
imitate them.

—James Baldwin
"Nobody Knows My Name" (1961)

The third mediation, *transcendence*, in addition to intention-
ality/reciprocity and meaning, is equally essential to all instructional interactions. An interaction that meets this criterion enables the learner to bridge from a here-and-now
learning experience to a grasp of the experience's underlying principles and value. When tied to intentionality, a transcendent mediation facilitates the learner's making connections with higher-order goals and purposes.

■ Student Opportunities for Making Generalizations

In the mediated classroom, the teacher provides multiple opportunities for the students to go beyond or "transcend" learning how to perform a task. She is more interested that they make generalizations or grasp the underlying principles about what they are doing. Preferably, she sets up a hands-on, laboratory-like situation that will provide a set of common experiences that will lead to the needed generalization. Take the concept of ratio, for instance. Rather than begin a lesson by giving a textbook definition of ratio followed by many problem examples and corrective feedback for mistakes, the teacher mediating transcendence will start the lesson by implanting the expectation of transfer and by providing a hands-on ratio experiment. In this case her immediate hands-on intention is for the students to understand how to perform *this* experiment; her *transcendent* intention is for the students to learn how to apply the principle of ratio when solving other problems in science, mathematics, or even social studies. How does she do this?

First, she will give each pair of students a cardboard tube from a roll of paper towels, a crayon, a tape measure, a pair of scissors, and a twelve-inch piece of string. She will show the pairs how to mark off the roll into thirds. At this point she will make explicit transfer back to check prior knowledge of "fractions." Next, she will invite each pair to use all hands to wrap the string around the tube and cut a piece of string of the measured length. Next, she will ask the students, "If you now stretch the string along the length of the tube, which line marked on the tube will the string reach?" After they test their guesses, she will show them that circumference (distance around the tube) is almost three times the distance across (diameter) and have them check this out once again with their strings.

After the pairs agree on this principle by checking out their own measurements, the teacher will give them other circular objects (glasses, cups, wooden dowels, plant pots, metal pipes, cans, etc.) to see if the principle holds. After the students have charted different examples, she will ask explicit questions to be sure they can explain why, with a variety of different circular objects they can visualize at home or in their community, the principle of ratio applies. If there are doubts, she will challenge them to test out the theory on other objects. Finally, using what they have observed in the experiments, she will help them form a generalized or "superordinant" concept called "ratio."

At this point, the students are prepared to do ratio problem solving with round objects. Although some might understand the principle well enough to solve a ratio problem with a square or rectangular object of different sizes, most would struggle with such a transfer challenge. To ensure success for all, she must devise enough additional concrete experiments with ratio that they can strengthen the generalization that allows them to see how ratio works regardless of size or shape. When these understandings are in place, she is then ready to cement the transcendent definition of ratio and to move the students to pencil-and-paper word problems.

A teacher of mathematics who feels forced to race through chapter after chapter in a textbook can argue, "I don't have time for all of these shenanigans. I have two days to teach ratio. I cover the text. They do the assignments. We move on. My job is to get those who can perform the tasks ready for the test. They either have the smarts to use what I taught or not. The time is not there for anything 'transcedent'." Such arguments strike right to the heart of the issue of transcendence. Time is important. However, if time is not allotted to develop deep understanding, the coverage of material in the textbook does little more than hide success from most students. They may memorize the formula; they may "get" the problems given, but without the understanding of the concept, future applications of the principle are iffy, especially when students are the episodic learners that many urban students seem to be. Ultimately, use of the textbook approach alone ensures that many students will leave school with a diploma but without the ability to connect ideas or events. To ensure that this doesn't happen, it is imperative that teachers selectively abandon the extraneous topics that force superficial coverage of the curriculum and take time to mediate in-depth understanding of the most critical concepts that are needed across the curriculum and in the world of work.

If time is not allotted to develop deep understanding, the coverage of material does little more than hide success from students.

■ Reciprocal Teaching

There are a variety of methods that promote transcendence. One of the most notable is a well-researched tool called *reciprocal teaching*. This method works in all disciplines that rely heavily on reading comprehension. Whether students must read from a math, science, or social studies text, decipher written instructions on a computer screen, or study a short story, the strategies learned in this approach will improve their comprehension and promote their ability to transfer new concepts through every discipline.

Reciprocal teaching starts with the teacher's introducing students to four reading comprehension strategies which help them read with the lesson's focus in mind and which are especially good at helping students remember what they have read. For each reading passage, whether it is instructional, expositional, or narrative, the students will learn *how to ask a generalizing question, how to summarize, how to clarify meaning,* and *how to make predictions.*

A *generalizing question* is one that focuses on the main idea of a paragraph or story. It is the opposite of a detail question that focuses on the facts. For instance, the question "What mark does a cheetah have under its eyes?"

is a detail question. The student can point to one sentence in the paragraph as the answer. On the other hand, a question such as "What kind of animal is the cheetah?" is a generalizing question—it requires several sentences as clues that point to the paragraph's main idea.

A *summary* is a concise explanation that captures all the details related to the main idea. For instance, a complete summary about how the cheetah protects her young would include several details such as "by whistling when danger is near," "by hiding them in the tall grass," and "by walking away alone from where they are hidden."

Clarification of meaning occurs when unclear referents, complex concepts, and abstract ideas are identified or when poorly organized material is explained. For instance, if a paragraph has overused the pronoun "she," the teacher might substitute where necessary "the mother cheetah."

The ability to make *predictions* demonstrates that students read texts with precision, draw correct inferences, and can anticipate what will happen next in a story or other selection. In a cheetah story, with students already aware of how the mother protects the cubs, students should be able to predict what will happen next in the passage when they learn that the cubs are threatened by the arrival of a lioness.

■ Implementing the Four Strategies

After introducing the four comprehension strategies with examples to the students, the teacher will inform them that she is going to model use of the strategies when reading a short story. First, she invites each student to read the first paragraph. When all are done, she asks detail questions about the paragraph and points out differences between the main idea and detail questions. Finally, the teacher summarizes the first paragraph and shows the students in detail how she made the summary.

As the teacher models use of the generalizing question and summarizing, she is careful to engage all of the students in the discussion (cf. the discussion of TESA, Chapter 2). She is especially careful to seek out random responses by calling upon students from all around the room. When an answer is given, whether it is correct or not, she respects the response. At the minimum, she says, "That was an interesting response, LaMont. Show me how you found it." Better yet, she listens for the part of the answer that was correct and points that out before calling for another student to complete the answer or give a different response. "I like the part of your answer that said . . . . Who can help LaMont with the other part?" When students are confused by unclear ideas, unusual and abstract words, or poor sentence structure, the teacher takes time to invite students to seek further summary or clarification, or simply to ask more questions. Once the summary is completed and the students seem clear on the main idea and the details, the teacher will model prediction making. She will ask the students to tell what they think will happen next in the story and ask them to explain the prediction based on what they have just read.

Once the first paragraph is done, the teacher will return to the definitions and ask the students to recall samples of each strategy which she used in understanding the first paragraph. After reminding students that reading in this manner is a group effort and that all are expected to work together in a respectful way, the teacher asks for a volunteer student to take her place in leading the discussion of the next paragraph. The teacher will continue this cycle for each paragraph; each time a new volunteer will lead, and the teacher will assist and review the four strategies at the end of each discussion. For each new paragraph, the teacher fades more into the background, saving her input for the end when the class reviews the strategies.

As a mediator of transcendence, the teacher directs the thinking processes in a supportive way. She is not telling the student how or what to think. Instead, as mediator, she provides the structure that refines the thinking process so that the student is using the process in an appropriate and logical manner. For instance, if the student creates a generalizing question for the paragraph, the teacher can provide support by asking, "Can you finish this question about the paragraph: 'What are the different ways that cheetahs _____?'" (e.g., protect their young). After the student responds with the organizing idea, the teacher mediates by asking, "Why do you think that is the generalizing question?" (main idea). If the student gives a detail statement ("She hides them in the brush") instead of a summary sentence ("She protects her young in several ways"), the teacher might say in a respectful tone, "Maria, you have selected a very interesting fact. Let's see what we can add to the sentence so that we have a more complete picture of the main idea. What else can you add from the paragraph? What do these sentences add up to mean?"

When students are having difficulty with words, the mediator may ask: "Are there some words in the third sentence that might give students of your age difficulty?"; "What words are not clear to you?"; or "Whose name would you put in place of this pronoun in the third sentence?" Such questions help students clarify the ideas and untangle confusions created by unclear syntax.

Finally, it is helpful for the mediator to ask questions that provide students with a pattern for making predictions in what they are reading. Research on reading comprehension has shown the importance of helping students become explicit predictors, noting that the strongest readers make predictions a natural part of their reading tasks—less able readers seem to lack a systematic way to do this. As discussed in the "mediation of meaning" sample lesson on making predictions (cf. pp. 45–47), the mediating teacher

As a mediator of transcendence, the teacher directs the thinking processes in a supportive way.

will increase all students' functionality as predictors. As more student-readers learn to improve their predictive ability, their reading comprehension will improve, not only in their daily work but on district, state, and national standardized tests as well.

To develop predicting skills for reading comprehension, the teacher-mediator will model a systematic method that the students can practice with each other in reciprocal situations; they will be able to go on and use this method on their own in any reading task in the curriculum (see the lists of reading materials from the sample lesson on making predictions, pp. 45–47). Instead of providing a complete text, the teacher will begin by doling the text to the students one paragraph at a time (refer back to the sample lesson use of "The Dinner Party"). After the students have read a paragraph, she will ask them one of two questions: "What do you think will happen next?" (for selections of fiction) or "What do you think the author will say next?" (for passages of non-fiction). After a number of students have declared their guesses (a guess is an unsubstantiated prediction), she will have the class pick the most likely predictions and then ask students to explain why. She will caution the students to limit their explanations to information provided in the paragraph just read. After hearing a number of rationales, she will distribute the next paragraph and repeat the question sequence. As she listens to the responses, she will not comment or judge. However, she will insist that all rationales come from the text, not from prior experience.

The teacher continues guiding practice until students show that they can use it without direction.

After the entire story or article is read, the mediating teacher will ask students to focus on the system that she used and to say what they may have learned about the system itself (the "system" is simply the two questions of "what do you predict?" and "why?"). The students have learned the systematic method of predicting from what they have read and how making predictions increases their attention to detail and main ideas and holds their attention in the reading process. After the first practice story has been modeled, the teacher can initiate the reciprocal process with pairs of students. Students will use other readings to ask each other the questions, to make their predictions, and to assess the prediction process. It is important that the teacher continues guiding practice of the process over several months until students show that they can use it without direction in a variety of academic disciplines.

After the teacher feels comfortable with students' use of reciprocal teaching, she may want to carry the strategy to the next step with an approach called "Fostering Communities of Learners." With this technique (advanced by Anne Brown, the researcher who devised reciprocal teaching), the teacher divides students into research teams. Using classroom materials or Internet resources, they seek information on a question posed to the entire class. Information is shared by using Aronson's cooperative learning strategy called the "jigsaw." In the jigsaw, once the groups have begun to gather information, group members disperse to other groups and share their infor-

IRI/SkyLight Training and Publishing, Inc.

mation. After the cross-group sharing, the class discusses the question using the reciprocal strategies of clarifying, summarizing, generalizing statements, and predicting with the mediating teacher's guidance. In pilot classrooms in San Francisco, Brown's research showed large and significant increases in comprehension, problem-solving ability, and reading performance.

To insure the bridging of the reciprocal teaching techniques and processes, it is important that the teacher remembers that the goal is student self-direction in using techniques to increase comprehension. Beginning with a direct instruction of the method, she will guide student use of the questioning strategies. When there is evidence that the students understand the process, she moves them to more independent practice in cooperative pairs. Ultimately, she sets up a challenge for each student to practice the reciprocal process. At this point, the teacher-mediator will take time to guide students to an understanding of the process and to explore other uses across the curriculum. As the school year progresses, she will provide explicit opportunities for students to practice and refine the reciprocal process. This last step ensures a high degree of transcendence. For students who are used to teacher-only direction of the reading process (i.e., only the teacher asks clarifying questions, predicting questions, etc.), it may be difficult to assume responsibility for asking peers these questions and becoming autonomous enough to ask themselves these questions when doing independent reading. For the transfer from teacher-centered questions to learner-centered questions to occur, the teacher-mediator must model and re-model, coach, and firmly support the students' efforts to master the strategies. It should not be surprising if students resist taking on this responsibility ("It's so hard to remember!" or "We didn't have to do this in Mrs. Smithson's class!" or "It's the teacher's job to ask questions!" are some of the whiny avoidance strategies the teacher may hear; pouting, goofing off in the pairs, or acting out in other ways are some of the "you can't make me" power strategies students will use). It is important that the mediator encourage students to work through their insecurities and live up to this high expectation for learning the process as well as the content of the reading task. The content will give them information; the process will enable them to make connections for a lifetime.

The experienced mediator can encourage students to stay focused on the reading strategies by preparing a bulletin board or providing a handout that lists the four reciprocal strategies with their definitions and patterns for asking each type of question. Whenever students get "stuck," the mediator can point them to the printed material for review. As students become more skilled in use of the reciprocal strategies, the mediator can increase the length or the complexity of the reading assignments. After each assignment, she will allow time to discuss the process with the entire class and for self-reflective journal entries that challenge the students to think about their use of the skills, how they are progressing, and the difficulties and concerns they

It is important that the teacher remembers that the goal is student self-direction.

are having. Eventually, with continued practice and support, the students be able to bridge the reciprocal strategies to complete fiction and non-fiction assignments in many different subject areas.

■ Recognizing Patterns

For the primary grades, learning about mathematical shapes is an important topic. Many workbooks end the lesson by asking students to match a shape with a word.

Match the Correct Shape

1. ○   _____ rectangle

2. □   _____ circle

3. △   _____ square

4. ▭   _____ triangle

A lesson designed to mediate transcendence goes beyond simple recognition of isolated shapes. It instead enables children to recognize each shape wherever it may be located. Notice how the lesson calls for explanations of the definition as the transcendence promotion method.

PRIMARY SCHOOL LESSON

Shapes

Problem
How to describe shapes in the world around us.

Focus Intelligence
Naturalist.

Supporting Intelligences
Logical/Mathematical, Visual/ Spatial, Interpersonal, and Bodily/Kinesthetic.

■ CHECKING PRIOR KNOWLEDGE

On the board, draw a circle, a square, a rectangle, and a triangle. Ask each student to think where he or she might have seen these shapes. Allow pairs to discuss the sightings before you ask individuals to share. Under each shape, list the appropriate responses.

■ STRUCTURING THE TASK

1. Break the class into four to six groups. Invite each group to form the shape you specify.

2. Invite the class to label each shape as you point to each example on the board. Ask "What makes this shape special?"

3. Give each group a worksheet with the four shapes. The groups will search throughout the room to find objects in which each shape is found. Let them write the object's name or sketch it.

4. Conduct a round robin and invite explanations/reasons for each selection.

■ LOOKING BACK

Invite each group to add an example to each list on the board. Conduct a round robin until all lists are complete.

■ BRIDGING FORWARD

Instruct each child to take a shape worksheet home so that they can find at least three items which contain each shape. Use the reciprocal model to check for understanding.

Assessing Student Performance

Each child can identify and name the shape within an object and can explain why each example is reflective of the definition.

Variation

Give each child a page of shapes to cut out and make a simple picture. Ask the child to explain *why* the picture is a specific shape.

❑ Formulating Principles

In the middle school lesson that follows, mediation for transcendence appears at two levels. First, the lesson asks the teacher *to bridge* from the poet's concrete description to other related experiences. Second, the lesson uses the reciprocal teaching model with this poem as a model. In addition, it asks the teacher to bridge forward the students' use of the model into other experiences. From this, the students are asked to formulate a principle for use of the model.

IRI/SkyLight Training and Publishing, Inc.

MIDDLE SCHOOL LESSON

"To the Young . . .": A Poem

Problem
How to transfer the meaning of a poem.

Focus Intelligence
Verbal/Linguistic.

Supporting Intelligences
Intrapersonal and Interpersonal.

■ CHECKING PRIOR KNOWLEDGE

1. Pair students together to read the Gwendolyn Brooks poem "To the Young Who Want to Die."

To the Young Who Want to Die
by Gwendolyn Brooks

Sit down. Inhale. Exhale.
The gun will wait. The lake will wait.
The tall gall in the small seductive vial
will wait will wait:
will wait a week: will wait through April.
You do not have to die this certain day.
Death will abide, will pamper your postponement.
I assure you death will wait. Death has
a lot of time. Death can
attend to you tomorrow. Or next week. Death is
just down the street; is a most obliging neighbor;
can meet you any moment.

You need not die today.
Stay here—through pout or pain or peskiness.
Stay here. See what the news is going to be tomorrow.

Graves grow no green that you can use.
Remember, green's your color. You are Spring.

2. Use a think-pair-share strategy to guide the discussion: "What do you think the poet is saying?" Use TESA skills to guide the discussion (cf. Chapter 2).

■ STRUCTURING THE TASK

1. After several pairs have shared their responses, explain to the students how to summarize the poem. (Do not model this poem. If you must model a complete summary, pick a different, easier example.)

2. Ask each pair to make a summary before you ask three to five different pairs to share. Give positive comments.

3. Write the word "clarify" on the board. Explain how the concept works with several samples from the poem. Invite the pairs to review the poem and ask about items that require clarification. Help the class respond and clarify.

4. Return to the whole poem and ask for students who want to change the summary to do so. Ask why and get their new ideas.

■ LOOKING BACK

Ask the pairs to respond to the poet. Do they agree or disagree with the final sentence? Why? Encourage listening to each other.

■ BRIDGING FORWARD

Review the strategies of summarizing and clarifying. If need be, repeat the process above with another poem for guided practice. When students demonstrate a heightened ability to summarize and clarify, make an independent practice assignment. Conclude your review by asking students to identify other opportunities to use these skills in school or at home and to form a generalized principle for their appropriate use.

Assessing Student Performance

1. Students can make an accurate summary of a short poem without assistance.
2. Students can clarify ambiguous items and weak associations in a poem.

Variations

1. Use a different medium, such as a short story, editorial, news clip, or short topic from the Internet.
2. Select a different poem.
3. Model both processes before using the poem.

■ Learning for a Lifetime

In the following secondary lesson, a single skill for improving reading comprehension is the focus. Without the mediation of transcendence, the lesson would end with the students bridging examples of what they learned. Note how the lesson leads up to "bridging forward" where the emphasis is placed on identifying transfers for the purpose of formulating a principle that will transcend all appropriate situations. Here the emphasis is on learning a principle that will hold true "for a lifetime."

What Is Next?

Problem
How to develop predicting skills as a tool that promotes advanced reading comprehension.

Focus Intelligence
Verbal/Linguistic.

Supporting Intelligence
Intrapersonal.

■ CHECKING PRIOR KNOWLEDGE

1. Select a novel or drama for an all-class study.
   Authors such as Hansbury, Baldwin, and Hughes provide strong literature adaptable to this strategy.

2. Present the title of the work selected. Ask a variety of students to predict what they think the work is "about." Probe for "why" and "honor" all ideas.

■ STRUCTURING THE TASK

Make the first reading assignment. Let the class know that after completing the first chapter assignment, you will ask only two questions. (Show on board.)

1. What do you think will happen in Chapter 2? Why do you think so? (Some of the responses will draw upon students' generalized past experiences with structure: "The first act introduces the conflict. The second . . . ." These are appropriate, but remind students that you are seeking specific evidence from the chapter just read that points to specific predictions about what's next.)

2. Solicit as many ideas as time allows. Assign each chapter, one at a time, followed by the two questions. As students make more accurate predictions, they will read more carefully to prepare for the next chapter and to see if they "got it"!

■ LOOKING BACK

1. As the work advances, call for chapter summaries. (You may need to review "how to.") At the end of the novel, call for a one-page summary of the novel or drama and review ideas from students.

2. Discuss how the two questions helped with reading comprehension.

■ BRIDGING FORWARD

1. Invite students to describe opportunities in school, at work, or at home in which they might benefit from making accurate predictions. Mediate "why" so that they will form a principle appropriate for use of this approach.

2. After the final summary, invite students to share lessons learned from the characters and how these lessons might benefit them at home, at school, or at work. Again, mediate "why" so that they can formulate the principle.

Assessing Student Performance

1. Each student will demonstrate how to ask the predicting questions in a piece of literature.
2. Each student will demonstrate how to respond to the predicting questions.
3. Each student will demonstrate the ability to apply use of the questions in three different situations.

Variations

1. Use a video of a play. Stop at key breaks and use the two question process.
2. Begin with a short story to model the process.
3. Instruct students to write individual essays as the bridging task.

The mediation of transcendence, coupled as it always is with *intentionality/ reciprocity* and *meaning*, is the theoretical explanation for the proverb "Give me a fish, I will eat for a day; teach me to fish, I will eat for a lifetime." When a teacher mediates transcendence for the urban child whose learning is often episodic and incidental, she provides that child with a powerful tool for the devlopment of the child's understanding. As the child learns to form principles that bind experiences, he learns why it is important to avoid life-threatening situations, why it is valuable to take advantage of schooling, and why ideas generated in school are part of a connected universe.

CHAPTER 5

Self-Regulation and Control of Behavior

The man who never
submitted to anything
will soon submit to a
burial mat.

—Nigerian proverb

For several decades, national surveys have shown that the public is most concerned about school discipline. In spite of a multitude of proposed solutions, ranging from the systemic approach of the effective schools movement to make the school a safe and secure place for all, to the more teacher-directed approaches of Driekurs, London, Jones, Burke, Denny, and other advocates of sound classroom management the concerns have escalated.

■ Discipline and Internal Motivation

Alfie Kohn attributes the failure (or the perceived failure) to correct the "discipline problem" to a misguided belief that "rewards and punishments" will change student behavior. As he notes in his writings, all of the most popular approaches to managing student behavior not only have a very low success rate (as evidenced by both the persistence and the growth of disruptive behavior) but also are not beneficial to students. In place of the common reward-and-punishment systems derived from the long-term influence of Skinner's behavioristic theory, Kohn advocates the development of systems and strategies that foster students' internal motivation.

It is the teacher's responsibility to mediate this self-regulation, not to impose punishment, dole out rewards, or ignore misbehavior.

Kohn's advocacy of internal motivation complements Feuerstein's belief in the importance of *self-regulation* and *control of behavior*. According to Feuerstein, only self-regulation leads students to take responsibility for their own behaving, learning, and thinking. Like other cognitive psychologists such as Ellis, London, and Dinkmeyer, as well as cognitive instructional strategists such as Costa, Brown, Barell, Musial, Hammerman, and Perkins, Feuerstein grounds self-regulation and control of behavior within the individual. As the individual "thinks about thinking" (metacognition), he constructs new ways of acting that lead to control of impulsive behavior, learns to break complex problems into small parts, and moves away from guessing how to behave toward a more systematic approach of self-discipline. In Feuerstein's systemic approach, it is the teacher's responsibility to mediate this self-regulation, not to impose punishment, dole out rewards, or ignore misbehavior.

Mediation of self-regulation and control of behavior occurs when the mediator interrupts impulsive and unsystematic behavior by asking the student to "stop and think." This makes the student conscious of the need to monitor and adjust what he is doing or thinking. As the student is rushing helter-skelter through a task or impulsively reacting to a situation, the mediator waves a stop sign in front of his eyes. This signals: "Stop your uncontrolled response. Look both ways. Recall the proper ways to react. Think about what you are doing. Proceed with caution."

■ Instrumental Enrichment

In urban classrooms where there are large numbers of students labeled "at-risk," ADHD, "learning disabled," "behavior disordered," "emotionally disturbed" (and on and on), the most advantageous way to introduce impulse control is through an intense, long-term program of Feuerstein's Instrumental Enrichment (IE). This gives teacher-mediators the opportunity to

IRI/SkyLight Training and Publishing, Inc.

establish a foundation of self-regulation without the distraction of course content. As many studies have shown, the most challenged students are no different than their high-performing peers: all students find it difficult to "think about thinking" when course content and subject matter are "what they are used to doing." In a high-action culture such as that in the United States, reflection is not a highly prized way of learning. IE requires that students learn to reflect, to stop and think, to plan and monitor what they are learning and doing, and to take responsibility for how they think and act. Mediation of this reflective behavior comes faster and easier without the added complexity of content. It also makes the ability to transfer across the curriculum and into other aspects of the students' lives much stronger.

There can be no question that an intense, structured program such as IE changes how students think and behave—more than 880 studies from nations around the world document that students can learn to regulate their own behavior. As this change occurs, attendance increases, referrals to the principal's office, fights, and other acting-out behaviors decrease, while achievement test scores, critical thinking test scores, and teacher-parent satisfaction increase. Two cases in point:

> In Taunton, Massachusetts, middle school teachers in the small urban system use IE with all students in an inclusive setting. In grades six to eight, each day starts with a full period of mediation. During the other class periods, teachers help students transfer what they have learned about self-control, systemic planning, and problem solving into each subject area. In addition, each subject area teacher mediates transfer of appropriate thinking skills into the various content areas, such as comparison and contrast in mathematics and categorization in science.

> In Omaha, Nebraska, principal James Gilg used IE in an alternative school. Earlier in his career, Father James Gilg had been the principal of a small inner-city Catholic-run high school designed to meet the needs of students who had experienced difficulty with formal schooling. Over time, Father Gilg became concerned that the school was merely helping these students find "success" by changing the school environment to meet their needs, instead of encouraging and initiating changes within the students to prepare them for challenges outside the classroom. In 1981, Father Gilg was introduced to Feuerstein's work in mediated learning. He discovered that IE allows students to find success in a real-world setting, helps them deal with more sophisticated issues than those typically found within the school walls, and enables them to become self-regulated, not just for the teacher but for a lifetime of work.

> In 1983 the school, Father Flanagan High School, adopted the concepts of mediated learning and began a systematic implementation of IE. All students were required to take IE as a separate course, and all teachers were trained in the program.

More than 880 studies from nations around the world document that students can learn to regulate their own behavior.

"The change in the school environment was very radical," said Father Gilg. "Through mediated learning, students' behavior improved, academic success increased, and students' awareness of thinking changed. IE also gave teachers a common vocabulary and methodology for teaching all of their classes."

Feuerstein's IE program is now being implemented around the world, from Madrid, Spain, to New Delhi, India, from Budapest, Hungary, to São Paulo, Brazil, from Israel to the Netherlands, from the United Kingdom to Mexico.

■ The Instruments in Feuerstein's System

Each of the fourteen instruments in Feuerstein's system focuses development of a specific cognitive prerequisite for learning. In addition, the continuous and intentional mediation of self-regulation enables the learner to decrease impulsivity and increase internal motivation for learning tasks even as they are learning how to learn more efficiently. There are fourteen instruments in Feuerstein's system:

1. Organization of Dots
2. Orientation in Space
3. Comparisons
4. Analytic Perceptions
5. Categorization
6. Family Relations
7. Temporal Relations
8. Numerical Progressions
9. Instructions
10. Illustrations
11. Orientation in Space II
12. Syllogisms
13. Transitive Relations
14. Representational Stencil Design

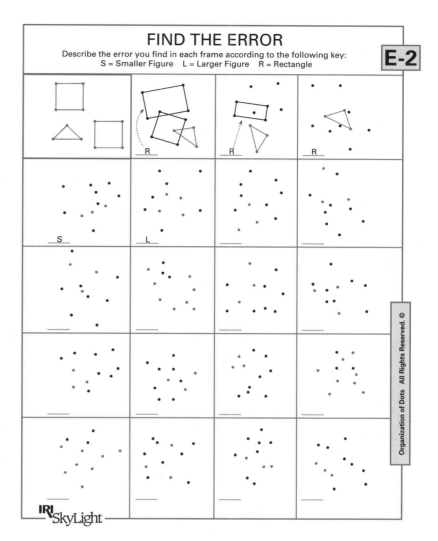

1. Organization of Dots.

The first and basic instrument calls for students to work with increasingly difficult frames of "dots." After organizing the first few frames, the mediator helps students construct the pattern used to connect the dots. Although different students report different sequences, all begin to see that they are most successful with patterning when they use a purposeful plan. As the students identify their own personal patterns, the mediator mediates use of the learned thinking pattern for the next, more difficult instruments. Success builds intrinsic motivation and the desire to attack the more challenging task. The mediator cues the students' metacognition by encouraging the planning and assessment of the increasingly difficult patterning process. It is here that impulse control becomes internalized and ready for application in the remaining instruments.

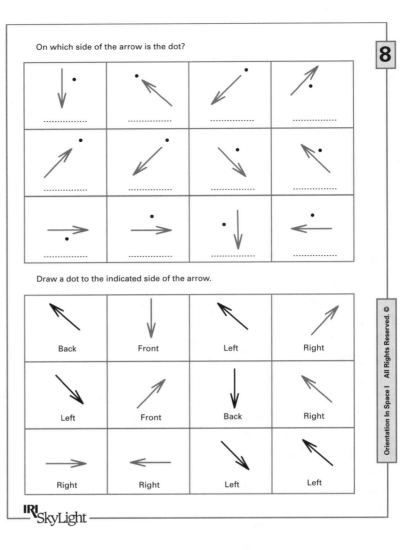

On which side of the arrow is the dot?

Draw a dot to the indicated side of the arrow.

Back | Front | Left | Right

Left | Front | Back | Right

Right | Right | Left | Left

2. Orientation in Space.

In his studies Feuerstein noticed the difficulties that low-functioning children experienced in locating their position in relation to objects. Where is right? Left? Up? Down? North? West? He devised a series of tasks which would challenge the students to find their place in space, even when familiar landmarks disappeared. The orientation in space instrument helps the children develop physical and abstract spatial relationships. It shows them how to use environmental clues and how to set direction. The gradation of instrument tasks from simple to complex allows the mediator to cue students on the gathering of directional information and the use of it to find their way first in concrete situations and then in conceptual problems. As the tasks increase difficulty, frustration can also increase. Intentional mediation of self-regulation, though, reinforces habitual self-control of behavior and thinking processes.

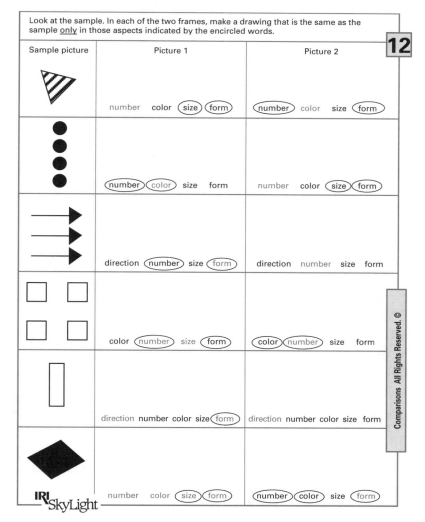

3. Comparisons.

It is popular in many classrooms to use Venn diagrams to help students note similarities and differences among characters in a story, periods of history, mathematical figures, etc. When students lack the foundational skill for identifying attributes of similar objects and for identifying differences, it is difficult for them to make meaningful comparisons. Feuerstein's third instrument helps students start with noting observable physical characteristics that denote similarities and allow identification of concrete attributes. As they proceed, the instrument presents more and more abstract comparisons. Noting how they think about comparisons as they move from concrete examples to abstract representation, the students build the cognitive structures they will need to work in content areas. As students learn to generalize the thinking processes inherent in comparisons, the mediating teacher helps the students transfer to a variety of subjects such as language arts (e.g., two characters), mathematics (two number sets), and social studies (two cultures). During the transfer process, students' frustration will likely intensify, since the learning transfer is taking place in unfamiliar and difficult territory. Once again, the mediator will bring the students' attention back to self-regulation as needed.

4. Analytic Perceptions.

When students weak in their ability to see the differences in geometric shapes approach their first geometry assignments in math, they encounter immediate failure. Unable to differentiate parts in the whole picture or confused by how to connect parts into a whole, the world of shapes and figures appears as a meaningless mish-mash. With this instrument the mediator helps students become proficient in recognizing geometric forms, thus freeing the students to distinguish foreground images from background shapes. As students develop multiple strategies for seeing and manipulating shapes, they become ready to perform geometric calculations in mathematics, develop systems for gathering information in completing complex tasks, eliminate trivial trial-and-error behaviors in favor of planned actions, and acquire precision and accuracy in relating parts to the whole. In addition to the obvious transfer into geometry, this instrument transfers into all situations where planning is important, including the assembling of machinery, the construction of furniture or buildings, the development of planning charts, the analysis of literature, and the drawing and reading of maps.

By this point students have spent three to five hours a week for thirty weeks working on instruments, developing thinking patterns, applying these patterns to their daily coursework, monitoring their own impulsive behaviors, and learning how to plan the completion of complex tasks. Impulsive behavior becomes more subtle and individual; this growing subtlety requires that the mediator have sharp eyes and ears along with strong intention in identifying students' impulsive thinking and acknowledging their ability to control their impulsiveness.

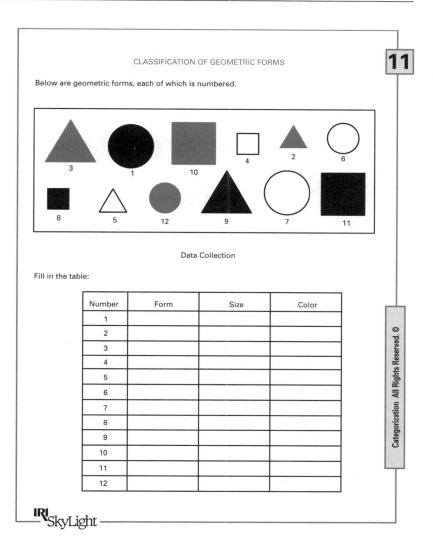

CLASSIFICATION OF GEOMETRIC FORMS

11

Below are geometric forms, each of which is numbered.

Data Collection

Fill in the table:

Number	Form	Size	Color
1			
2			
3			
4			
5			
6			
7			
8			
9			
10			
11			
12			

IRISkyLight

5. Categorization.

This instrument helps students build on comparisons (instrument number 3) by focusing on the classification of information. Starting with items that are familiar to them (sinks, faucets, fences, flowers, trees, dogs, birds), students learn how to use precise verbal labels, gather data in an orderly fashion, compare similarities and differences, select the relevant qualities of an item, and place it in the most precise cognitive category. As students improve their ability to categorize concrete items successfully, they are presented with new items of increased abstraction. On the affect side, the mediator assists students in restraining impulsivity by encouraging systematic exploration of possible answers and precise placement of objects in well-defined categories. Transfer tasks range from helping students organize their desks to categorization tasks in science, social studies, and English grammar.

6. Family Relations.

This instrument uses the metaphor of "family" to mediate students' ability to make connections or see relationships. Feuerstein selected
the family metaphor because of the wealth of emotional experiences that it provides as prior knowledge. This richness expands the possible number of valid generalizations that students can create about the thinking process of "seeing connections."

Above you see a diagram of a family.
Such a diagram is called a genealogical map. The map is blank (empty).

Place the names in the blank genealogical map, as indicated by the following sentences:

a) Arthur is Rita's father.

b) Simon and Jerry are brothers.

c) Jerry is Laura's son.

Answer the following questions with the help of the map.

a) Who is older, Rita or Laura? _____

b) Who has two brothers? _____

c) Who has a brother named Simon and one sister? _____

Complete:

a) Arthur and Laura are the _____ of _____.

b) Arthur and Laura are _____.

c) There are more _____ than _____ in the family.

d) There are more _____ than _____ in the family.

IRI SkyLight

Starting with a discussion of the possible ways students are related to other people, the mediator helps students form generalizations about how other objects in their world of experience are related or connected. The mediator can then move the students to apply the generalizations to academic subjects. In this way the mediated instrument leads to the breaking down of the very common student perception that "English is not math; math is not social studies; and social studies has nothing to do with science." As the students develop their connection-making ability, they become better able to integrate what they are learning (including impulse control) across the curriculum.

7. Temporal Relations.

Telling time seems like an easy task. However, when children don't have digital watches or clocks, the task becomes slightly more difficult. When time-telling problems go beyond the immediate twenty-four hours, children who have never mastered the mysteries of duration and intervals must struggle to know what time it is. Starting with an examination of time intervals and relationships (e.g., sixty seconds to the minute) as a hierarchical structure, the seventh instrument helps students explore other differentiated hierarchies that involve dynamic continua that require temporal orientation (e.g., the seasons, inferred events). The mediator works to facilitate student planning and thinking through goal-setting and achieving behaviors and to enhance the use of plotting tools such as the continuum, the matrix, and the chart. When students have completed this instrument, it is anticipated that each will have built a framework for diagnosing complex temporal relationships—this ability will transfer into studies of historic timelines, units of measurement, and the analysis of time-dependent information in such fields of knowledge as geology, anthropology, and literature.

19

Complete the sentences below using one of the following three words:

time, distance, speed

1. We measure _____ with a watch.
2. We measure _____ with a speedometer.
3. We measure _____ with a tape measure.
4. We say "60 miles (96 km) per hour" in order to indicate _____.
5. We say "three hours" in order to indicate _____.
6. We say "50 miles (80 km)" in order to indicate _____.

To the left of each sentence, indicate whether it describes time, distance, or speed.

_____ A racing car can travel 200 miles (320 km) per hour.

_____ In order to reach New York City, one has to travel 300 miles (480 km) from Washington, D.C.

_____ In order to reach Paris from New York, one has to fly for about eight hours.

Write a sentence describing the speed of a car.

_____

Write a sentence describing the distance between two places.

_____

Write a sentence describing the time that has passed.

_____

IRI SkyLight

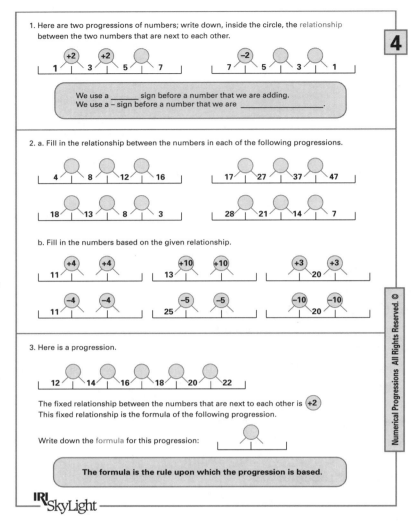

8. Numerical Progressions.

How many high school math teachers face students whose computational skills test at a third- or fourth-grade level? In spite of years of remediation, these students have not improved their basic skills; as the years pass, they stay frozen on the third-grade plateau. Such students exemplify Feuerstein's category of "retarded performers." In this case their stymied performance was preceded by a "glitch" in the formation of the cognitive basics needed to advance mathematical performance.

This instrument attacks the fundamental problem that impedes math mastery. The glitch is called "the episodic grasp of reality." When young children do not receive the meditation that enables them to see connections between events, facts, or ideas, they may master the first math basics by rote and by guess. When faced with more complex number tasks, such as adding or multiplying in tens and hundreds or following a sequential number pattern, they are at a loss. Without understanding the rules and laws that govern a succession, students cannot construct new number sequences, see recurring patterns, or predict new order. In short, without this understanding, math that goes beyond children's ability to memorize is impossible. By repeating instruction in the "how to" of addition, subtraction, multiplication, and division without helping students understand the principles of numerical progression, the teacher has little chance of improving the students' mathematical performance.

One of the main goals of this instrument is to help students discover the connections among facts and concepts. In this way they form patterns of thinking that reduce their episodic grasp of experiences and events in everyday life and increase their ability to deduce relationships among increasingly complex items and concepts and to solve problems.

DIAGONAL

17

1.

Diagonal lines
(Slanted lines–neither
vertical nor horizontal)

A diagonal in a polygon

2.

The diagonal in the rectangle
connects the _____ right
corner with the _____
_____ corner.

The diagonal in the rectangle
connects the _____ right
corner with the _____
_____ corner.

3.

In the square, draw a
diagonal that will connect the
upper left corner with the
_____ corner.

In the square, draw a
diagonal that will connect the
upper right corner with the
lower left corner.

4. Draw a diagonal in each of the figures. The diagonal should start from the upper right corner.

5. Does the diagonal BISECT the figure? (Bisect = divide into two equal parts) Circle the correct answer.

Yes/No   Yes/No   Yes/No   Yes/No   Yes/No

®SkyLight

© 1996 R. Feuerstein, HWCRI, Jerusalem. Instructions

9. Instructions.

One of the chief difficulties students have in school is their inability to follow instructions. The causes of this are numerous. Sometimes impulsivity and lack of planning are the culprits; in other cases, students may lack the ability to discover or coordinate the most important parts of an instruction; still others lack the ability to put instructions into a precise sequence. The instructions instrument returns the students' attention to geometric shapes. They are given written instructions to describe and construct drawings that coordinate number, size, color, location, and direction. This process requires cooperation with another student, as one works to give precise instructions and the other to follow. To complete the tasks, the students must form hypotheses and use logic as they seek alternatives for carrying out an instruction.

The transfer possibilities for this instrument are obvious. The mediator's task is to help students use their increased understanding of instructions in test-taking situations, work situations, and the completion of projects.

10. Illustrations.

A popular graphic organizer used by business teams is the fishbone diagram, developed in Japan by Ishikawa for use in analyzing cause-and-effect and for making judgments about connections between means and ends. For instance, in the auto industry work teams searching for the causes of common car defects have used the fishbone to track down the problem; this sophisticated tool let these users arrange the relevant clues that showed the real causes of the defect rather than leaving workers to repair superficial dents and scratches on each car as it came off the assembly line.

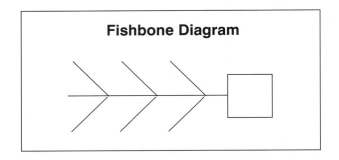

Fishbone Diagram

In order to work with the fishbone diagram, the problem solving process requires advanced and very subtle thinking skills. Most important is the need for the problem solver to have refined inferential skills. As the national data on reading comprehension reveal, making inferences is one of the most challenging and one of the least developed skills in the preadolescent and adolescent population.

Before students can succeed with a cause-and-effect thinking task, even one made easy by a fishbone diagram, they must have the capability to make simple inferences. If this capability is weak, Feuerstein's *Illustrations* instrument becomes

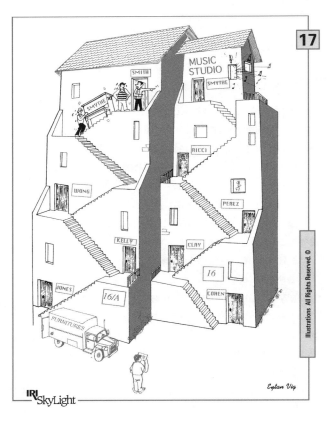

a prerequisite. Using humorous illustrations, the instrument introduces the important relationships between affect and cognition. Building on skills developed in other instruments, illustrations sharpen inductive and deductive reasoning, improve decoding of information, promote divergent thinking, and teach students how to extrapolate information in order to synthesize facts into an integrated concept connecting causes with effects.

From the perspective of transfers, this instrument has multiple values. Most importantly, it improves students' ability to make inferences. Starting in the fourth grade, inference-making is the critical skill for strengthening reading comprehension. As students experience the content-free, fun challenge of visual inference-making, the mediator guides them in using the process for making inferences about literature, science, and mathematics. In addition, as the students' inference-making becomes stronger, they become better at diagnosing cause-and- effect in literature, social studies, applied mathematics, and science.

IRI/SkyLight Training and Publishing, Inc.

11. Orientation in Space II.

Orientation in Space II extends students' ability to use absolute external and stable points of reference so that they can describe their own relationships and location in different spatial dimensions. It provides intense practice with the use of compass points, coordinates, and spatial graphs and challenges students to see relationships in differentiated representational space. This instrument also gives the mediator the opportunity to reinforce planning behaviors for use in solving complex geometry problems.

1. Write the directions in the rectangles.

NORTH

14

2. Where will you be?

A. You are facing west. Make 6 turns to the right and 2 left turns.
   Where do you face now? _____

   [6] − [ ] = [ ]   Equal to _____ turns to the right

B. You are facing southeast. Make 6 left turns and 2 right turns.
   Where do you face now? _____

   [ ] − [ ] = [ ]   Equal to _____ turns _____

C. You are facing southwest. Make 10 turns to the right and 2 left turns.
   Where do you face now? _____

   [ ] − [ ] = [ ]   Equal to _____ turns _____ or a _____ circle

D. You are facing south. Make 5 left turns, 3 right turns, and 6 left turns.
   Where do you face now? _____

   [ ] − [ ] + [ ] = [ ]   Equal to _____

E. You are facing southeast. Make 8 right turns, 2 left turns, and 3 right turns.
   Where do you face now? _____

   [ ] − [ ] + [ ] = [ ]   Equal to _____

F. You are facing southwest. Make 3 right turns, 2 left turns, and 5 right turns.
   Where do you face now? _____

   [ ] − [ ] + [ ] = [ ]   Equal to _____

®SkyLight

© 1996 R. Feuerstein, HWCRI, Jerusalem. Orientation in Space II

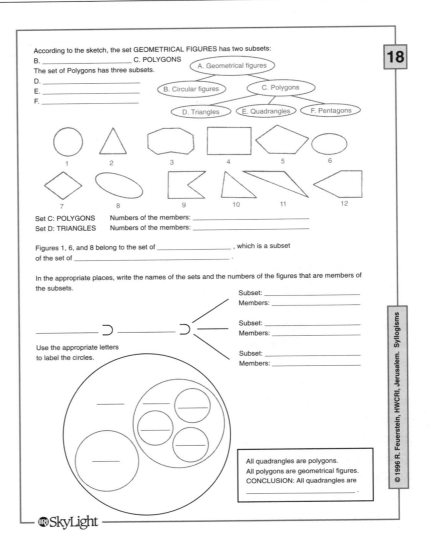

According to the sketch, the set GEOMETRICAL FIGURES has two subsets:
B. _____ C. POLYGONS
The set of Polygons has three subsets.
D. _____
E. _____
F. _____

A. Geometrical figures

B. Circular figures   C. Polygons

D. Triangles   E. Quadrangles   F. Pentagons

1   2   3   4   5   6

7   8   9   10   11   12

Set C: POLYGONS   Numbers of the members: _____
Set D: TRIANGLES   Numbers of the members: _____

Figures 1, 6, and 8 belong to the set of _____, which is a subset
of the set of _____.

In the appropriate places, write the names of the sets and the numbers of the figures that are members of
the subsets.

Subset: _____
Members: _____

Subset: _____
Members: _____

Use the appropriate letters
to label the circles.

Subset: _____
Members: _____

All quadrangles are polygons.
All polygons are geometrical figures.
CONCLUSION: All quadrangles are

_____.

®SkyLight

18

© 1996 R. Feuerstein, HWCRI, Jerusalem. Syllogisms

12. Syllogisms.

When the title of this instrument is given, many wonder how students who can't pass a basic skills test can operate in the world of logic. Logic, after all, has long been associated with the private domain of gifted thinking and philosophers.

This advanced instrument relies on the cognitive foundations established with previous instruments to develop a particular type of reasoning by which students draw logical conclusions. The instrument begins by introducing the concept of "set" as a well-defined collection of items. As students proceed through the instrument, the mediator helps them learn how to define the limits of a set, to draw conclusions based on simple deductive arguments, to distinguish between universal sets and subsets, and to provide practice in drawing conclusions about the connections among sets. Finally, the mediator has the opportunity to use the Venn diagram as a tool for transfer not only in identifying sets (as done with literature, math, social studies, etc., elsewhere in the instrument) but also as a tool for establishing logical arguments.

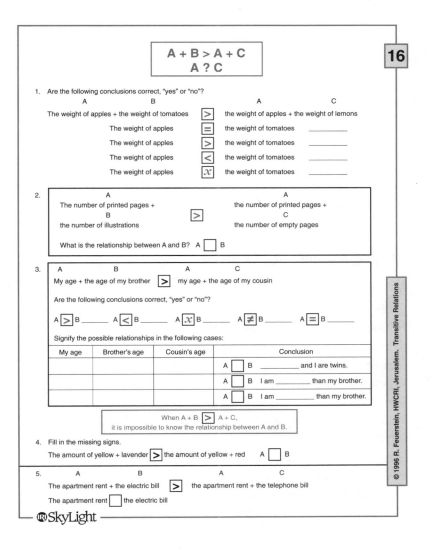

13. Transitive Relations.

Algebra is an obstacle that keeps many students from proceeding into advanced mathematics. Without getting past algebra, the gate to higher education is closed. This instrument extends students' ability to learn and apply the principles of logic begun in Instrument 12 *(Syllogisms)* and uses the new understandings so that they can learn how to form equations. This instrument introduces the concepts of "greater than" and "less than" by working with concrete examples such as the ranking of people by age, height, weight, and size and the ranking of places by area, population, age, housing units, etc. From these examples, students form generalizations that the mediator helps them apply to day-to-day experiences. Finally, students use the instrument's tasks to learn about signs, symbols, and equations and about how to seek the information that allows them to transfer relationships in an equation.

14. Representational Stencil Design.

One of the most complex thinking tasks that blocks students from thinking in complex ways is the forming of hypotheses. Using representational stencil designs, this instrument provides students with the skills to form and test hypotheses. As they are challenged to do "what if?" thinking in order to solve design problems, the students begin to extend the flexibility of their thinking. In order to succeed at the challenging tasks in this instrument, students must increase their comfort zone for taking conceptual risks. The mediator helps by facilitating the students' recourse to their prior knowledge of problem solving as this knowledge was developed with the previous instruments. In addition, the mediator helps the students with hypothesis-forming tasks drawn from science, mathematics, and social studies.

---

1. Look at the poster and fill in the blanks.

   Solid square ___red___ Number _____
   Solid square ___white___ Number _____
   Solid square _____ Number ___1___
   Solid square _____ Number ___5___
   Solid square ___yellow___ Number _____

   The solid squares are all found _____.

2. Square number 10 is _____.

   On the poster there are two more green squares which are cut out inside.

   a) The form which is cut out of the center of number 11 is _____.

   b) The form which is cut out of the center of number _____ is _____.

3. On the poster are four white squares: one is _____ and three _____ inside. List the number and the form of each of them.

   a) Number _____ Form _____
   b) Number _____ Form _____
   c) Number _____ Form _____
   d) Number _____ Form _____

4. List the colors and the numbers of the cut out squares.

   Color: _____

   Number: _____

   Color: _____

   Number: _____

   The squares that are on the poster are called STENCILS. On the poster there are _____ stencils that are solid, and twelve stencils that are _____.

1

© 1996 R. Feuerstein, HWCRI, Jerusalem. Representational Stencil Design

®SkyLight

Use of Instrumental Enrichment on a daily basis produces numerous results, including cognitive improvement and academic achievement, that are measureable in a number of ways; the first measureable effects, however, come only with behavioral change. When the mediator of self-regulation adds other methods to the use of the instruments, these effects are increased.

☐ Mediating Self-Control

The first method that extends students' capacity for self-regulation is helped by explicit social skills lessons that focus on the values of self-control.

MIDDLE SCHOOL LESSON

Exercising Self-Control

Problem
How to increase self-control and avert impulsive behavior.

Focus Intelligence
Intrapersonal.

Supporting Intelligences
Interpersonal and Visual/Spatial.

▓ CHECKING PRIOR KNOWLEDGE

1. Show the class a picture of a STOP sign. Ask them to describe its purpose and its importance. ("Cars stop" and "prevents crashes", "injuries," etc.).

2. Ask the students to reflect on "invisible" STOP signs which tell us to stop what we are doing. Make a class T-chart for those signs and their importance.

Signs	Importance

▓ STRUCTURING THE TASK

1. Select one of these tasks to help groups of students illustrate one invisible "stop sign" story:

   a. draw a cartoon story

   b. act out a play

   c. sketch what happens when the sign is ignored.

   Assign the students into groups of three with an encourager, recorder, and checker. Set the timelines and walk among the groups to ensure that all contribute.

2. Post the completed products around the room.

▓ LOOKING BACK

1. In the days following, select one invisible stop sign. Ask the group responsible for it to share their ideas. What is the sign? When is it important to use? Why is it important? When was a time it worked? What happened when someone ignored the sign? Ask each group to demonstrate how the stop sign helps them regulate and control their behavior.

IRI/SkyLight Training and Publishing, Inc.

2. Post the chart below on a bulletin board. Explain the words and record each group's responses:

	The Sign	Use	Reason	Plus	Minus
1.					
2.					
3.					
4.					
5.					

3. After each group has shared and discussed with the class its generalization, ask the following: "What does the chart tell us about stop signs? Why are they important? How do they help us?" Use extending questions to deepen understanding.

■ BRIDGING FORWARD

Use students' learning logs. Invite each student to select one "stop sign" for personal use in the next day, week, or month. (Designate the time in accordance with student readiness.) Have each student describe how she will use her personal stop sign. Each day allow five to ten minutes for students to record successful uses of the personal stop sign (competence). Coach and encourage as needed. To further mediate competence, follow the log entries with a few public "sharings." Use random selection. Celebrate each success with a "hurrah!"

Assessing Student Performance

To what degree can the student:

1. Explain why stop signs are important?
2. Name "invisible" stop signs?
3. Use "invisible" stop signs to control his or her impulsivity?

Materials

Stop sign picture, T-chart, art supplies, student journals.

Variations

1. Invite students to identify situations when they can fail to control their own behavior. Have small groups role-play on the consequences of poor impulse control.

2. Create classroom PMI charts (Plus-Minus-Interesting Questions) on your modeling of various situations calling for impulse control.

P	
M	
I	

3. Make TV ads for impulse control on important situations.

Once students begin to demonstrate evidence of conscious self-regulation, as shown by the alignment between talk and actions, it is appropriate for the mediator to weave mediational phrases throughout the school day. This mediation will address not only overt behavior but also task- and problem-solving behavior.

Overt Behavior

TEACHER: "Today, class we are taking a trip to the library. Which of our rules do you think will apply? Margarita?"

MARGARITA: "Listen to the person in charge. She will explain what we can do."

TEACHER: "Thank you. Are there other ideas? Tomas?"

TOMAS: "Yes. We need to respect each other."

TEACHER: "Why do you think that?"

TOMAS: "Because it helps us pay attention to each other and not distract each other."

TEACHER: "Does the respect rule always apply?"

TOMAS: "Yes, when we are with people."

TEACHER: "How do we show respect? Susan?"

SUSAN: "By the way we stop and think and by not interrupting or distracting each other."

TEACHER: "This is a difficult math problem. How should we begin? Missy?"

MISSY: "We should stop and think about our plan."

TEACHER: "That is a good start. Who can give me the plan? Mildred?"

MILDRED: "We have to set our goal. Next, we have to see what is given and plan a strategy. Once we have a strategy, we pick our starting point."

TEACHER: "A good start, Mildred. Who can carry on? Michael?"

MICHAEL: "We have to review the rules and check our work."

TEACHER: "I liked how we made our plan first. Now you are ready to start. What is our goal?"

☐ Other Self-Regulation Strategies

In many urban schools around the globe, Instrumental Enrichment has proved a powerful starting tool for teaching students how to control their own behavior. However, it is not the be-all and end-all—it is one means to the end of having students develop an internal locus of control for how they regulate their behavior and the quality of their thinking. The mediational strategies that teachers use with students in IE are valuable tools for helping the students transfer their new habits of thinking across all curricula and outside the classroom. Likewise, other strategies help teachers mediate self-regulation even without the benefit of full IE implementation. Here are some other mediational strategies:

- create with the class a motto (such as "Think First") to guard against impulsivity;
- create a bulletin board that celebrates step-by-step planning of school tasks;
- create in small groups a series of poster-ads to hang around the room or in the hallways. Each poster can use the class motto and show different situations where it helps to "think first";
- model self-control by not interrupting students' answers, by using wait time, and by saying aloud "Just a moment, I have to think about that" before answering a student question;
- when students finish a task, allow several minutes for them to review and check their work;
- brainstorm with the class on ways and times to forestall impulsivity;
- in cooperative groups, make a T-chart of how one acts and speaks when forestalling impulsivity. Set up individual contracts with de-layed impulsivity goals and self-assessment of improvement. Once a week, discuss what improvements are occurring;
- teach students how to use graphic organizers to plan decisions and chart sequences of procedures;
- require students to have an assignment book. Take ten minutes at the end of each day to enter homework assignments. Use paired partners to check each other's entries;
- make daily use of the think-pair-share strategy;
- record on the board with a sequence chart the steps students took in solving a problem. In algebra, insist that students can show the step-by-step procedure for solving an equation;
- each day before collecting homework, ask students to evaluate the quality of their work against a set of criteria that you keep posted in the room;

- assign activities in which students must rank their activities by order of importance and defend the choices made;
- provide students with blank weekly or monthly schedules and use paired partners to fill in the schedules with all out-of-school responsibilities;
- ask students to break a complex task into its component steps and then to put those in a sequence for which they can explain the rationale;
- use cooperative groups to construct maps showing safe alternative routes for students to take to and from school;
- discuss the value of thinking first and postponing action;
- acknowledge students who take the time to reflect before giving an answer;
- use journals to ask students to write down answers to thought-provoking questions. Tell them ahead of time that they may have the opportunity to share aloud;
- encourage students to take time out when they feel that their emotions are getting out of control;
- use journal entries that encourage students to track how they are improving in self-control;
- with the students, develop classroom behavior guidelines that focus students on self-regulation. Post the guidelines and refer to them as needed.

Self-regulation runs contrary to much of the behavior urban students see on TV crime stories and in gang outbursts; other sights and sounds of the world in which they live reinforce impulsive actions, too. When the teacher mediates self-control, especially in conjunction with transcendence, isolated acts of planning, goal-setting, and sharing take on new meaning. These new meanings enable students to understand the value of self-control, especially when learning, and transfer that value into action.

Competence

Once I get the ball,
you're at my mercy.
There's nothing you can
say or do about it. I own
the ball, I own the
game. I own the guy
guarding me. I can
actually play him like a
puppet.

—Michael Jordan

When mediating *competence*, the teacher or parent purposefully instills a belief in the student about his ability to succeed. Furthermore, the mediator helps each student turn this belief into a lasting motivation to try increasingly difficult tasks. The mediation of competence differs from the practice of "cheerleading" for immediate effects.

☐ The Mediation of Competence

A mediator uses strategies that will result in long-lasting effects. These strategies enable the student to grow increasingly persistent in overcoming obstacles and succeeding against tougher and tougher odds. The competence-building strategies require that the mediator walk a fine line between establishing goals that can be attained and mediating challenges through the provision of novel and difficult tasks. This makes the mediation of competence a process of continuous improvement, based on the student's growing perception of inner growth, accomplishment, and progress.

Teachers in urban classrooms are likely to encounter many students who feel incompetent, and there are many reasons why such students feel this way. In some cases, the feeling may be present because of continued low expectations. In the home, a child's parents may take a laissez-faire or hands-off attitude; they let the child sit in front of the TV, or mope around the apartment, or talk endlessly or purposelessly on the phone, or roam the streets. "So what if he doesn't read? I didn't when I was his age" or "I don't have time to check his homework" are responses typical of low parental expectation. As parents model these low expectations, the child frames his own low expectations. Here, the self-fulfilling prophecy starts to work, and the child is soon saying to himself, "I am not much good at (fill in the blank), so why bother?"

> Feelings of incompetence may start with overdemanding parents who are never satisfied with their child's level of achievement.

In other cases feelings of incompetence may start with overdemanding parents who are never satisfied with their child's level of achievement. The child, responding to perfection-demanding parents, brings home a report card with five As and a B. The parent rages: "How could you get a B? You're a disgrace!" The child, ashamed but desiring to meet her parents expectations, becomes convinced that her failure to get six As was worse than the success she achieved in the five courses. Thus, she sees herself as incompetent.

The successful mediator of competence learns to recognize the behavioral indicators that suggest strong feelings of incompetence:

- refusing to start tasks, lack of perseverance, finding ways to avoid tasks, acting-out impulsively, missing assignments, or delaying the start of a task;
- talking the "victim" language: "It's not my fault"; "She made me do it"; "I can't"; "It's too hard";
- showing increasing anxiety: tears, shaking hands, looking at floor, stomach pains, feigned injury, headaches;
- increased patterns of avoidance: late or missing homework, tardiness or absence, frequent requests to leave the room, acting-out to force punishment or expulsion

IRI/SkyLight Training and Publishing, Inc.

- perfectionism: overworking an assignment, compulsive practicing, overattention to what others think, excessive competitiveness, sleeplessness;
- undue exaggeration: bragging, bravado.

Feelings of incompetence are not an either-or phenomenon. They are best viewed on a spectrum that is balanced against actual performance.

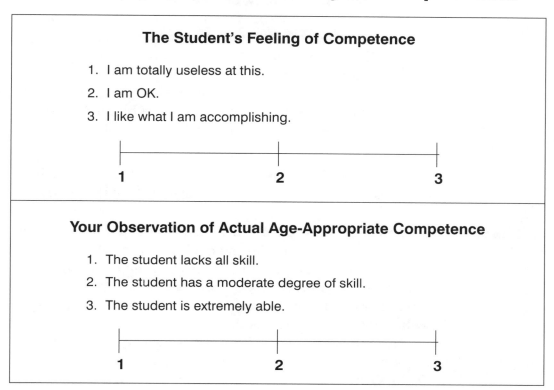

The Student's Feeling of Competence

1. I am totally useless at this.
2. I am OK.
3. I like what I am accomplishing.

1   2   3

Your Observation of Actual Age-Appropriate Competence

1. The student lacks all skill.
2. The student has a moderate degree of skill.
3. The student is extremely able.

1   2   3

In school, it is academic competence that needs to be the focus of attention. Within the academic arena, the student may have a feeling of incompetence that coincides with a very low skill and knowledge level, or she may have a feeling that does not accurately reflect what she is able to do. Consider these two instances:

1. Juan moved from Central America to a suburb outside a mid-western city. Although he knew only a few English phrases, the school assigned him by age to a sixth-grade class. As he sat in the classroom, he could not follow the lessons in English. Frustrated, he began arriving at the bus stop after the bus had departed.

2. Toshan's parents had very high expectations. In the early grades she had shown a special gift for math and science. At home, her parents provided her with science kits, played math games with her on the computer, and tutored her in advanced mathematics. In the ninth

grade, her mathematics teacher invited her to join the math Olympics team. Toshan's parents were thrilled and hired a coach to tutor her in advanced algebra and geometry. Preparing for her first competition, Toshan practiced each night until two or three o'clock in the morning. She devoted her weekends to further practice.

Toshan's first competition was a disappointment. Because of her quickness, accuracy, and knowledge, the sponsor had placed her on the varsity team; but matched against older competitors, she froze at each question. Although she had been able to answer far more difficult questions in the team's practice, she failed to answer any in the competition.

Afterwards, when the coach attempted to discuss her performance, Toshan burst into tears and blamed herself for failing to study more. She promised to rededicate herself and do a better job preparing for the next tournament.

In each of the two examples above, competence is the central issue; each case is different, however. Juan came up with an avoidance strategy, being late for the bus, as a way to handle the frustration generated by his feelings of incompetence. His feelings matched the reality of the situation. Without the language skills, he couldn't undertake the classroom tasks performed by the other students. Toshan settled on self-blame followed by a "work harder" response. Her feelings of inadequacy were based on the wide gap between what she believed she had to do to be perfect and the high skills she already possessed.

> In spite of what self-esteem gurus advocate, there is not a magic cure-all for feelings of incompetence.

In spite of what superficial self-esteem gurus advocate, there is not a magic cure-all for feelings of incompetence or of low competence. As with all blocks to learning, the skilled teacher will construct mediation strategies that match individual need. When students lack competence in a specific academic area and feel incompetent, lessons must be designed that include the most productive instructional strategies. Foremost among these strategies, as shown by three decades of research, is TESA (Teacher Expectations and Student Achievement—cf. Chapter 2).

■ TESA

The TESA project found a clear connection between what teachers expected of students and the resulting performance. Just as Rosenthal had noted in his classic study "Pygmalion in the Classroom": "What you saw was what you got"—and this is what Kermin found to be true in the Los Angeles classrooms where teachers followed their beliefs that poor, minority students couldn't learn.

IRI/SkyLight Training and Publishing, Inc.

What were the teacher behaviors (and the expectations they evinced) that Kermin and his associates found to have the greatest impact on children in the classroom? There were fifteen which became the heart of the TESA training program.

1. *Equitable Distribution.* Thomas Good's research (1987) had shown how teachers tended to call more often on students who sat in the front row and middle seats in the classroom (the T) and ignored students outside the T seating pattern; students in the back corners had the least likelihood of being asked to answer a question. Moreover, by the middle grades, many students learned the strategy of distribution and sat themselves, given the choice, according to their desire to participate or not participate. High performers went to the T, low performers to the corners.

   To correct the unequal distribution of questioning, TESA taught teachers to make a conscious effort to direct their questions to the corners and the back of the room. When put into effect, the strategy put students on notice of the expectation that all students, regardless of seating, would have an equal chance to be called on. There would be no hiding in a TESA classroom.

2. *Affirm/Correct.* In his 1981 study of teacher behavior, Good had noted that teachers gave less accurate and less detailed feedback to students they perceived as low achievers, giving students perceived as high achievers more detailed and accurate feedback. He also noted that Anglo students were more likely to get accurate and detailed feedback than Mexican American students. Rubovits and Maehr (1973) had noted a similar pattern when black and white students were in the same classroom.

   In the TESA project, teachers were trained to make accurate comments about each student's response. The feedback would note that an answer was correct or incorrect and, in the best circumstances, would explain "why."

3. *Proximity.* Using a variety of research studies, the TESA project showed how the teacher's physical closeness to the student affected time on task. In the project teachers learned how to reseat students, how to rearrange seating for easier access, and how to move closer to students who were off-task.

4. *Individual Help.* Sadker and Sadker (1985) noticed how the assertiveness of high-achieving students, especially males, resulted more in individual help. In the TESA project, teachers learned how to identify the two or three students who received the least amount of attention, even when they called for help in a proper manner.

5. *Praise.* Rosenshine (1972) and Good (1981) both documented how teachers were less likely to praise perceived low achievers for academic performance and more likely to praise perceived high achievers. Moreover, researchers noted that teachers tended to protect low achievers from criticism about wrong answers. The TESA project trained the teachers to give energetic, positive feedback and rewards to all students, with a special concentration of attention for the perceived low performers.

6. *Wait Time.* Mary Budd Rowe provided the research that showed the importance of teacher silence after asking a question. She noted how often teachers answered their own questions or jumped to a new question in less than eight-tenths of a second. She also noticed how student involvement increased when teachers extended the wait time or silence to two or three seconds. In the TESA project, teachers were trained to keep quiet for two or more seconds, to not answer their own questions, and to not add additional questions.

> The TESA project trained teachers to give energetic, positive feedback and rewards to all students.

7. *Courtesy.* A number of researchers, including Brophy, Good, Hillar, Sadker and Sadker, and Rist, have observed that many teachers were discourteous and disrespectful toward "low-status students" yet demanded that those students show respect to them as teachers. More often than not, high-status students, those who received the most attention from the teacher, copied the teacher's behavior toward the low-status students. This included interrupting answers of the low-status students, high use of put downs, and sarcasm. The high-status group members were mostly white males; minority females were the lowest status group.

   In the TESA project, teachers were taught to identify how they created or contributed to high- and low-status groups by the way they gave attention, responded to students with courteous statements such as "thank you" and "please," and avoided the use of sarcastic tones and belittling phrases.

8. *Reasons for Praise.* After helping teachers in the project change their patterns of praise (see item 5 above), the project deepened their understanding of how offering reasons for praise corresponded to the equal distribution of status. Brophy (1986) had already noted that many teachers gave fewer reasons for praise to low achievers; teachers tended to give low-status students "static" praise which was overdone and simplistic, such as "Good job," "Yes," and "OK." When teachers distributed praise and provided reasons, Brophy noted a change in students' achievement.

   TESA trainers prepared teachers to follow Brophy's criteria for giving praise at selected appropriate times, such as when a student

IRI/SkyLight Training and Publishing, Inc.

would make a genuine and significant gain or when a student would fail to appreciate her own progress. The trainers also provided criteria for judging the quality of praise. These criteria included the notions that sincere praise is appreciative, responsible to a specific accomplishment, natural, private, and attributed to effort and ability.

9. *Personal Regard.* Brophy (1986) observed that teachers in his study paid less attention in academic and social situations to the socio-economically disadvantaged students. The more advantaged students received more smiles, more eye contact, more questions that asked them to connect academic content to personal experiences, and more positive responses to personal examples. Outside of class (as in the lunchroom or on the playground), teachers gave less time and attention to the personal well-being and interest of disadvantaged students.

   In the TESA project, teachers in training learned how to develop content-related questions that connect to what they knew might be of interest to a student. For instance, a science teacher might ask Raphaela to explain how water temperature affects her swimming; a social studies teacher might ask Juan to compare the means of transporation used in his native Mexico to the means used in Los Angeles. In neither case would the teacher limit these interest-connected questions to select students. The teacher's challenge with these questions and other displays of personal regard is equitable distribution.

10. *Delving.* Brophy (1986) had also noticed how low achievers were asked fewer and easier questions than high achievers. If the low achiever showed signs of bewilderment, the teacher more readily turned to another student or answered the question. When high achievers were questioned, the teacher more readily gave clues, probed for evidence or reasons, or encouraged a more extensive response. TESA teachers were trained to push students to expand on their answers, to ask all students a second or third follow-up question that forced them to delve more deeply into course content, and to provide clues that would help all students, especially the lowest performers, to give a full response.

11. *Listening.* In 1971, Flanders noted how teachers spent more time talking to low-status students and less to the high achievers. In contrast, perceived high achievers spent more time sharing ideas, conversing with the teacher, and engaging in activities that required student talk.

12. *Touching.* Relying on studies that showed how a teacher resting a hand on a student's shoulder or forearm was more effective in focus-

ing a student's attention on a task than simply reprimanding or talking to the student, the TESA project researchers anticipated later learning style research that identified the needs of kinesthetic learners for physical contact. (Obviously, this research also antedated unfortunate classroom incidents which have made any touch by a teacher an act to avoid or to be very cautious about.)

13. *Higher Level Questions.* TESA brought to the forefront the issue of lower- and higher-order thinking as expected of low- and high-performing students. The researchers noted how low performers were limited to factual questions: who, what, when, where, and how. High performers were given the questions that asked them to process, apply, and evaluate ideas. To counter this tendency, TESA prepared teachers to use tools such as Bloom's taxonomy of cognitive objectives to frame the complete range of questions for all students. In this way teachers would communicate that all students were expected to perform complex thinking tasks.

14. *Accepting Feelings.* TESA research distinguished between a teacher's indifferent response to a student's task performance and the teacher's acknowledgment of the affective dimension of the student's performance or response. For instance, with less effective feedback the teacher would acknowledge minimally that the student had given a correct answer; with more effective feedback, the teacher would acknowledge the joy or pride with which the student had communicated the answer or response. If the teacher had to give corrective feedback, she would also acknowledge the student's disappointment. When this occurred consistently in a classroom, students were more open and responsive to feedback from the teacher and consequently more likely to act on improving and/or correcting their work.

15. *Desist.* In high expectation classrooms, the TESA study described how teachers maintained on-task behavior by directly confronting off-task behavior. This direct confrontation identified the specific misbehavior, expressed the teacher's feeling about it, and instructed the student to stop the misbehavior and replace it with a specified acceptable behavior. In contrast, teachers with low expectations allowed students to continue misbehavior and often justified what the students were doing with statements of low expectation such as "what else can you expect?" or by increasing voice volume to a scream.

The chart on the facing page describes a positive "desist" strategy that shifts responsibility to the student.

TESA prepared teachers to communicate that all students were expected to perform complex thinking tasks.

Tell Me

"_____ (student's name), tell me what you are doing."

There are a variety of answers possible:"Nothing"; "They made me"; or "I was _____ ." If the answer is "Nothing," try humor: "Only rocks do nothing—are you a rock?" or identify the behavior: "I saw you _____ . Was I seeing things?"

Next ask, "What are you supposed to be doing now?"

The answer should be quick. If the student says, "I don't know," give him time to think it over, to read the class's behavior guidelines, or to ask someone else for help. The student must respond.

Third, ask, "How do your actions help you do your assigned job?"

This question may evoke silence or a creative avoidance answer with which you must disagree.

Finally, ask the student to decide on a new behavior, "Are you ready to _____ (expected behavior)?"

If the answer is "No," give the student time to reflect. If the student says "Yes," then indicate that he may return to the task only if the new behavior is used. As soon as the misbehavior recurs, the student takes time out. Outline the conditions for return: *(a)* "When we can agree how you will be-have" and *(b)* "you show it."

After the student returns to the class from time out, keep a watch for the student's acceptable behavior. Give the student special recognition for the new positive behavior. Ask a mediating question that has the student assess his behavior.

When a student is sent from the group for time out, set the time out conditions and determine a policy for return. As an alternative to working in the time out space, allow the misbehaving student the option of being a classroom observer.

The value of TESA strategies should seem obvious, but in the bustle of a busy classroom, consistent and appropriate use is not easy. Pressured to cover a topic quickly before a bell rings or distracted by unforeseen interruptions, a teacher can easily rush questions, call on the first students that respond, or ignore partial answers. Once students with feelings of incompetence experience teacher behaviors that communicate low expectations, they begin to adapt themselves to the easier demands. If a teacher is noted for calling on those sitting in the front row only, those who feel incompetent soon learn how to hide in the back row; if the teacher never waits for their answers, the students learn how to clam up.

IRI/SkyLight Training and Publishing, Inc.

PRIMARY SCHOOL LESSON

Out of the Magic Hat

Problem
How to think before we act.

Focus Intelligence
Verbal/Linguistic.

Supporting Intelligences
Intrapersonal, Visual/Spatial.

■ CHECKING PRIOR KNOWLEDGE

Ask students to think of a time when they acted before thinking. Tell them "no hands" and to first think for a minute (wait time). After that time, ask for a sample of answers (equally) and *delve* or *cue* as needed.

■ STRUCTURING THE TASK

1. Introduce your "magic hat." Ask each child to print or write her name on a 3" x 5" index card, fold it over, and put it into the hat. Mix the cards up.

2. Explain the purpose of the hat: to pull the names of students so that everyone gets to answer some questions. Set the guideline "no hands to answer."

3. Ask the next think question: "Why is it best to think before acting?" Use the hat after a minute's wait. Delve and cue as needed.

4. Repeat with two other questions: "When are some important times to think before you act?" and "How are you going to become a more careful thinker?"

■ LOOKING BACK

On the following day (using the hat, wait time, delving and cuing again), ask: "What was a way yesterday that you stopped and thought before acting?"

■ BRIDGING FORWARD

Give pairs of students a sheet of art paper and crayons. Tell them to plan a picture showing a time or place it is best "to stop and think." Model as needed. Post the finished work.

Assessing Student Performance

Students show increased comfort with wait time.

Variation

1. Close with a role-play by trios. Each play will demonstrate a "stop and think" incident.

2. After a month or so, eliminate the hat.

IRI/SkyLight Training and Publishing, Inc.

MIDDLE SCHOOL LESSON

Who's the Leader?

Problem
To identify the qualities of a positive leader.

Focus Intelligence
Interpersonal.

Supporting Intelligence
Verbal/Linguistic.

■ CHECKING FOR PRIOR KNOWLEDGE

Ask each student to recall a person who was a strong, positive leader. (Allow wait time.) What were their characteristics? Write their answers on the board or overhead (equal distribution, delving, affirm and correct).

■ STRUCTURING THE TASK

1. Explain characteristics as personality traits or attributes, as the pieces of personality that help make each of us unique. (Give an example from history or your family life of such unique characteristics.) Note that some characteristics define personalities who become famous leaders. This unit will look at the characteristics common to leaders and examine how students can learn to develop some of these.

2. Divide the students into trios. Assign a recorder, manager, and checker to each trio. Review the jobs of each.

3. In turn, invite each trio to brainstorm the characteristics of the leader picked in the focus activity. The recorder will write down each new characteristic and asterisk the duplicates.

4. Each trio will select its top three agreed-upon characteristics and develop a reason for each choice. The checker will ensure that everyone in the trio can explain the choices.

5. Instruct each trio to split into three and join a new trio. Reassign the roles. Have each new trio compare its selections with the others. Identify similarities.

6. Ask recorders to report on similarities found. Record these on the board or overhead.

■ LOOKING BACK

Clarify in discussion the identified similarities. Seek examples of these qualities in action. Ask students to explain how the same characteristics might help them in a critical situation. (Identify TESA behaviors you will use to guide this discussion.)

■ BRIDGING FORWARD

Provide students with one of the seven following scenarios. In their base groups the students will review the positive leadership characteristics and develop two role- plays. In one, the trio will show how the characteristics helped; in the second, they will show how not employing the characteristics led to disaster. Allow one class period for planning and practicing. On succeeding days, allow the groups twenty minutes each for (a) their presentations and (b) discussion of the examples as they relate to real situations.

Scenarios

1. Three students are invited to a party at a good friend's house. While there, five other uninvited friends arrive and bring beer.

2. You are at a school party. The older student who drove you gets drunk.

3. Your teacher gives you an assignment for homework that requires library research. To get to the library, you must cross a gang's turf. Neither you nor your friends belong to the gang.

4. On your basketball team are two players whom you overhear talking about smoking dope. As a team member who took the oath, you are bound to report what you heard.

5. You are invited to a party after homecoming. At the party you see the team captain doing crack.

6. On a school bus trip, a parent chaperone offers wine.

7. Your best friend tells you that she's pregnant but doesn't want you to tell anyone.

Assessing Student Performance

1. Each student can identify three leadership qualities.

2. Each student selects one quality to develop.

Variation

1. Share one or two scenarios and invite students to create their own.

2. Invite each group to compose a popular song about leadership. Share these (affirm, praise).

SECONDARY SCHOOL LESSON

Egg Toss

Problem
To understand how one develops a sense of competence.

Focus Intelligence
Bodily/Kinesthetic.

Supporting Intelligences
Verbal/Linguistic, Interpersonal, and Intrapersonal.

■ CHECKING PRIOR KNOWLEDGE

1. On the board, construct a T-chart titled "Competence." (Practice wait time, equitable distribution, praise.)

Competence	
Looks Like	**Feels Like**

2. Ask for a number of volunteers (equal distribution) to give personal examples of what competence looks like and/or feels like. Record these.

■ STRUCTURING THE TASK

1. Let the class know it will play a game to test its hypotheses in the T-chart (be sure to have given advance notice: old clothes will help).

2. Take the class outside and set up two paired lines. Give each pair a water balloon. At your signal, call for the first toss and catch. Encourage partners to coach each other.

3. After each round, add another foot between the two lines. The winning team will have the most distance and be the least wet!

■ LOOKING BACK

Invite pairs to think about answers to these questions. (The Hat described in the primary lesson will help wait time.) Practice the TESA behaviors:

How did it feel to keep dry with catches and tosses with greater distances?

How did you try to help your partner?

How did it feel when your balloon broke?

What do you think is the competence lesson here?

■ BRIDGING FORWARD

Discuss this question as you use your TESA skills: What lessons did this activity teach that you can use in school or out-of-school situations?

Assessing Student Performance

Students can relate feelings of competence to their own lives.

Variations

1. Use a different game familiar to students, such as "rock, paper, scissors," "Frisbee toss," or "knots."

2. Conclude by asking each student to write an essay on "a competent person I know."

A student who feels incompetent may do so in one academic area or in all. The mediator cannot allow these students to escape or hide. What the teacher/ mediator can do is increase her repertoire of competence-enhancing behaviors and strategies so that step by step the students begin to see what they can do, because they are mediated to succeed.

Sharing Behavior

> It wasn't necessary to
> kill the Indian. If we
> were going to steal the
> country, we could at
> least [have] shared it.
>
> —James Baldwin

In our high-speed, high-tech world, information bombards adults and children with overwhelming intensity. Faster and more powerful computers process in a single day more new data than were generated in all of the first millennium A.D. The more the data flow, the less likely it is that the volume of information can be processed single-handedly and the more likely that individuals will feel the need to work with others. Thus emerges the increased emphasis in business, government, and other work areas for teamwork.

■ Advocates of Sharing Behavior

Feuerstein believes that sharing behavior is "one of the foundations of our social existence" (Sharron 1987). Sharing behavior occurs when a group of learners works together to achieve a common goal. When the mediator works with students to mediate any learning goal, she models the sharing behavior which will enable her to collaborate with students so that they can develop sensitivity to others.

Feuerstein's psychological emphasis on sharing behavior parallels the work of social psychologists Roger and David Johnson, Robert Slavin, Elizabeth Cohen, and other advocates of cooperative learning. For Feuerstein, sharing relates to the intrinsic need for interdependence. The mediation of sharing behavior helps children form the friendships that facilitate communication and break down egocentric behavior, loneliness, and emotional isolation. To accomplish this, as Feuerstein learned in his work with the children of the Holocaust, the mediator creates an environment of trust in which to strengthen students' self-concepts, promote experiences of accomplishment, listen with empathy, and clarify confused and cloudy thinking. For the Johnsons cooperative learning provides a powerful tool for building positive interdependence among individuals with a shared goal. As the Johnsons' extensive research has shown, this positive interdependence, coupled with individual accountability, taught social skills, and the assessment of teamwork in the completion of face-to-face tasks, improves student achievement, self-concept, and critical thinking more successfully than other models of instruction.

Cooperative learning provides a powerful tool for building positive interdependence.

■ Sharing Behaviors in the Home and Family

In a home rich with mediation, early sharing behavior is nurtured through the parents pointing at, singing to, playing with, and modeling for the child. From the parent-dominated activities in the first years of life, sharing behavior increases interactivity as the family develops give-and-take dialogues at the meal table, while watching television, when completing chores, or when shopping at the store.

When the child enters school, she may have her first experience of learning to share with peers. Given the opportunity to work with a peer or complete a problem-solving task with a group, students continue to grow in their ability to show empathy and develop more complex social relationships. Most importantly, they learn how to work in a team to accomplish a task that they could not perform alone.

In some urban classrooms children arrive without any notion of sharing behavior. If they have grown up as street survivors without strong early mediation for sharing, they may come to school ready to do battle to the death. They know street survival, where "look out for yourself," "don't trust anyone," and "save your own neck" are the learned behaviors. In school this translates to "me first, last, and always," "after me, you can be first," "I'll do it my way," and "be reasonable, do it my way." These youngsters know how to trust only themselves. Any overture to build trust and friendship must be actively rejected.

In his work with the children of the Holocaust, Feuerstein confronted a similar set of street-survival beliefs. He had seen these children fight for scraps of food in the ghettos; he knew that many others had lost their lives through the deception of fair-weather friends. He understood the depth of pain which grew from their need to take care of themselves, and he grasped the necessity of mediating how to share. Thus, sharing behavior became the gate which, once opened, could most readily admit these children to the world of learning. And just as Feuerstein succeeded with mediating sharing behaviors to the children of the Holocaust, he argues today for their mediation with urban children who come to school isolated and alone.

☐ Strategies for Developing Sharing Behaviors

In the past two decades, the proponents of cooperative learning have developed a multitude of easily implemented strategies that enhance sharing behavior in the classroom. These methods are as simple as a teacher's offering encouragment to students to help and listen to each other, to be sensitive to each others' special needs, to give examples of sharing behavior, and to stop behavior that offends others in word or deed. Alternatively, sharing strategies may be as complex as use of the jigsaw, problem-based learning teams, base groups, or peer editing pairs.

Consider the following examples:

Think-Pair-Share

The Think-Pair-Share strategy is one of the easiest tools for devloping shared behavior in a classroom. It has many uses. The Think-Pair-Share strategy can be used: to begin a new topic or unit by having students discuss prior knowledge; after a lecture, to help students summarize key points; to stimulate student thinking about an important piece of information; to check students' understanding of or insight into a topic; to bring closure to a lesson; to deepen students' short-term memories; or to promote student transfer of a concept.

With each of these uses of the think-pair-share strategy, give similar instructions:

Before the task: "Today I am going to describe _____ (topic). After I define each term, I'm going to ask you to _____ with a partner." To fill in the second blank in this statement, select one of the following: *(a)* summarize the key points, *(b)* tell what you already know about the topic, *(c)* pick one idea of importance and explain it, *(d)* tell how the information is important, or *(e)* tell something new you learned about the topic. After ten to twenty seconds, sample student ideas for the whole class.

After the task: "Turn to the person on your (right/left side), and take turns _____ " (see *a–e* above). Allow two to three minutes for each person to share.

Know Your Role

Knowing and assuming roles are important keys to successful teamwork in any group task. Roles are the first ingredients in preparing students for bonding, for being accountable for the whole group's work, and for assessing the group's performance.

Explain Why

The simple strategy of getting students to explain reasons for their answers is yet another effective means of building sharing behavior. This strategy enables students to rehearse their reasons for selecting an answer. Before a lesson, ask groups of students to discuss three to five multiple-choice questions that check prior knowledge. After each question is answered, invite several group reporters to explain *why* the group selected those answers. Solicit several answers to each question, write them on the board, and then discuss the merits of each answer.

Business Cards

The "business card" is another motivational rehearsal tool that involves the entire class. Give each student a 3" x 5" index card. Explain that the purpose of a business card is to present or introduce each other.

Model the following instructions on the overhead or board by giving sample answers to the following:

A. write down your first name in the middle of the card using capital letters (e.g., TOM);

B. write the name of your school beneath your name (e.g., Benjamin Banneker Middle School);

C. write in the upper right hand corner of the card a *success* you have had this week at school, home, or play (e.g., made a friend, got a score of 95 on a quiz);

D. write your *learning goal* for this week in the lower right hand corner (e.g., improve vocabulary quiz score, finish a paper);

E. write a *benefit* of doing your homework in the upper left hand corner (e.g., higher grades, improved self-esteem);

F. write down a *favorite book title* in the lower left hand corner (e.g., *Miss Nelson Is Missing, Freedom Songs, Who Is Carrie?*);

G. name your best cooperative skill (e.g., listening).

After all students have completed their cards, instruct each one to find a partner. After the pairs settle, instruct them to focus on one of the corner topics (success, goal, benefit, or favorite) and explain *why* that topic was selected. After one or two minutes, instruct students to switch partners. Continue switching until all the students have discussed all four of the corner topics on their business cards.

We Bags

Give each pair of students a paper bag. Invite the pairs to decorate them with their own names, the names of their favorite books or foods, or the names of places they have visited. Then have the pairs fill their bags with objects that have special meaning to them. Students should prepare to introduce their partners by discussing each item that is in the bag. Match the pairs into foursomes to introduce their partners.

"I Learned" Mail-Gram

For rehearsal after a lesson, invite each student to complete an *"I Learned" Mail-Gram*. Pass out cards with the "I learned . . ." stem. Have students fill in and sign the form. Next, match students into pairs to share the mail-grams. Rotate the pairs several times.

Vocabulary Jigsaw I

Select nine vocabulary words. Divide the class into trios. Give each group member three words and instruct each student *(a)* to learn the definitions of the words, *(b)* to draw a sketch of each word's meaning, and *(c)* to use the sketch to teach the other group members in a round-robin teaching. In fifteen minutes all members must know the meaning of the three words they've been given. To help, have the checker quiz the other group members after each round of three words and for the nine words total before you quiz each student:

Get Ready: review your roles and the task;

Step 1: learn the three words and draw a picture of each word (using it to teach the other members);

Step 2: conduct the first round of teaching and check (having each member review the definitions), coaching as needed;

Step 3: second round of teaching and checking;

Step 4: third round of teaching and checking;

Step 5: groups double-check;

Step 6: quiz;

Step 7: elicit a group list of learning strategies used (checking after each round; making and explaining a sketch; giving encouragement; etc.).

T-Chart

The T-chart consists of two columns, one column headed "Looks Like" (what the topic *looks like* is listed in this first column) and the second headed "Sounds Like" (with what the topic *sounds like* listed in the second column). Explain that the lesson at hand will now demonstrate the use of this kind of chart. The T-chart is used to help pairs of students clarify concepts or ideas and to help each other give specific examples.

Cooperation	
Looks Like	**Sounds Like**

What? So What? Now What?

Another chart that helps develop sharing behaviors is a three-columned chart that includes:

What?	So What?	Now What?

IRI/SkyLight Training and Publishing, Inc.

What?

In the "What?" column students in pairs or trios organize various ideas they want to discuss at a conference and identify an accompanying artifact from their portfolio that will help them explain their points. These are listed as topics, but issues, concerns, or focal points serve as well.

So What?

"So What?" dictates a processing response that sheds light on why the topic or concern is included. Typical processing statements that students address as they think about the "So What?" column are: why it (the topic) seems important; why it seems relevant; why it seems weak or strong; or what it represents or signifies.

Now What?

"Now What?" brings the reflection to meaningful application ideas. This is where the students project how the topic (or idea) is useful, connects to other things, can be modified, or perhaps might be of use to others.

While this is only one of many organizers, it seems particularly useful in helping students reflect and prepare for a conference because the three questions proceed from simple information through more personal and more meaningful justification to future application.

Story Element Web

After students have read a story, provide each group with an element web. Instruct them to complete a story element web. Assign roles and review responsibilities.

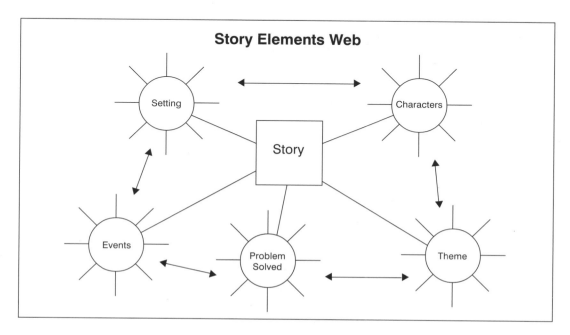

Math Practice Teams

After explaining and demonstrating a new skill (such as adding fractions), use teams of two or three students each to practice/coach through examples. Check for understanding as you monitor the groups.

☐ Cooperative Team Skills

In addition to using cooperative strategies that promote sharing behavior and student achievement, it is important also to develop students' cooperative team skills. The more skilled students become at working together, the more they will develop the sharing behaviors necessary for a learning community in which all students are respected and included.

When students come to school without the social skills that will enable them to do well, it is necessary for the mediator to set lessons that allow time for teaching the skills explicitly. After an introductory lesson, the teacher can begin to infuse what the students have learned to do and to say into subsequent lessons on a daily basis by asking students to assess their use of the new social skill. For instance, in the primary lesson that follows, the students learn how to show respect. After this lesson, the teacher can use mediating strategies such as a daily class round robin: "I'd like each one in turn to complete this stem: 'Today, I showed respect when _____ .'"

What's in a Name?

Problem
How to use names in school.

Focus Intelligence
Interpersonal.

Supporting Intelligence
Intrapersonal, Visual/Spatial.

■ CHECKING PRIOR KNOWLEDGE

Ask students: Why do we have names? Elicit multiple responses. Next, introduce yourself by printing your name on the board (e.g., Mr. John Smith). Sound out your name and have the class do a choral reading with your direction. Invite them to call you by your title and last name.

■ STRUCTURING THE TASK

1. Explain to the class how important it is to call people by their names and that in this lesson they will learn each other's names.

2. Assign each child one-third of a "people card." Each third of a people card has on it a colored dot (red, green, or yellow) and a letter. Tell the children to find the two other parts of their people card (same letter, different colors) so that they will form groups of three. (Show a model group of three and count off each child in the group: "One, two, three.") In the group of three, all must have the same letter and three different colored dots. (Show red, yellow, and green.) Signal the class to start. As groups of three are formed, instruct those groups to sit down together. Help those who are having difficulty until all groups are seated where you want them.

3. Invite the children with the red pieces to come to the materials table and pick up a sheet of newsprint and some crayons.

4. Each child is to sketch a self-portrait on the sheet. Be sure that the groups decide whether they are all going to sketch at once or take turns. They may help each other, but they may not offer any "bad talk" about each other's sketches. (Some examples of bad talk are: "That looks dumb"; "That's stupid"; or "Mine is nicer than yours.")

5. As they are drawing, give each child an index card (with the child's first name printed on it) and a piece of tape. If some children cannot print their own names, someone else may, or else they may affix the index cards to their sketch.

6. Invite each group to stand up. As the students with the red and yellow dots hold the newsprint, the students with the green dots will introduce all three of their group members. Encourage the class to give each group applause or a hurrah after its introduction. Post the completed sketches.

IRI/SkyLight Training and Publishing, Inc.

■ LOOKING BACK

Ask class members how they felt working together on the task. Encourage a variety of students to respond. If they start to repeat each other's responses, ask for the next one to think of a different word to descibe how he was feeling.

■ BRIDGING FORWARD

Give each child an index name card to wear for the rest of the day. Sit the children in a circle. Invite the children to share their names as they show their cards. After a child has shared his name, lead the class in a choral answer to the following: "What is his name?", "His name is _____." Emphasize that you want them to call each other by the given name.

Materials

Index cards, colored dots, newsprint, crayons, masking tape.

Variation

Repeat the name circle each day until the children form the habit of calling each other by their first names. For variety, have team members introduce each other. Ask only the question "What is his name?" without modeling the response. You may want to see how many classmates each student can name. For this, have a volunteer walk behind the circle and name each child in turn. When the child misses a name, he sits down and another volunteer takes over.

In addition to teaching explicit social skills lessons, the teacher can mediate sharing behavior by setting up classroom structures that enable students to develop interpersonal skills helpful for creating a community of learners (Senge 1995).

IRI/SkyLight Training and Publishing, Inc.

PRIMARY–MIDDLE SCHOOL LESSON

Social Skills/ Forming Friendship Circles

Problem
How to enable all students to form school friendships.

Focus Intelligence
Interpersonal.

Supporting Intelligence
Intrapersonal, Visual/Spatial

▨ CHECKING PRIOR KNOWLEDGE

1. Place the students' chairs in a circle. Read a story or relate a personal incident about the importance of friends.

2. On the overhead screen or blackboard, build a spider map on the importance of friends. Use a wraparound (with the right to pass), inviting each student to contribute to the map. Help by clarifying and ensuring that each student is heard.

3. Invite several students to summarize the ideas.

▨ STRUCTURING THE TASK

1. Give each student a copy of "Your Circle of Friends" and invite each one to fill in the diagram privately.

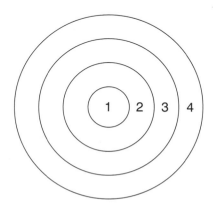

2. Circle 1: those closest to you, that you love and can count on the most (i.e., family).

3. Circle 2: those you like and can trust (i.e., school friends).

IRI/SkyLight Training and Publishing, Inc.

4. Circle 3: those with whom you like to do things (i.e., sports team).

5. Circle 4: those who get paid to help you (i.e., doctor, teacher).

6. Without invading their privacy, ask students to compare how it might feel to not have anyone in circles one or two as opposed to having people absent in circles three or four.

7. Discuss what it means "to feel incuded."

8. Brainstorm a list of ways we can exclude a person, even by mistake.

9. Brainstorm and record ways to ensure that every student in the class is included in class and out-of-class activities.

■ LOOKING BACK

Ask students: "Think about a time you were excluded by an important other. In your journal, describe how that incident made you feel. How can that experience help you in the future?"

■ BRIDGING FORWARD

Give each student a 3" x 5" index card. Have each one write something she could do to help a classmate be included and on the other side of the cards to write one thing that others might do to include her in the future. Select several to read at random to the circle.

Materials

Your Circle of Friends worksheets, 3" x 5" index cards, student journals.

Variation

In the Bridging Forward: (1) ask students to write about how they can strengthen the bonds of friendship in their own homes; and (2) pair students who are not already friends and have them plan a project together.

In a learning community where sharing behavior is the norm, achievement soars. After mastering the basics of working and sharing with each other, students can learn to use the cooperative structures and strategies in a triple agenda. First, they improve the social skills that business and industry consider essential for employment in the next century. Second, they improve their cognitive skills and become problem solvers. Thirdly, they raise their achievement level in the content areas. To build on this triple agenda, the mediator uses lessons that integrate content learning with cooperative teamwork and critical thinking in lessons that challenge students, deepen meaning, and increase sharing behavior.

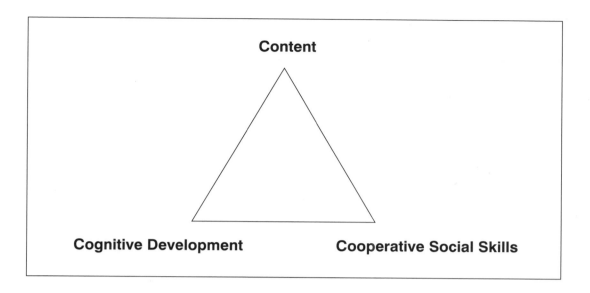

Throughout the activities and lessons that promote shared behavior, it is the mediator's responsibility to draw children's attention to ways of sharing that are helpful, ways that are not helpful, and ways to improve. The strategies and structures that the mediator plans create a context for sharing behaviors. Her interventions call students' attention to understanding why they are sharing. She helps them construct this understanding and to benefit from the positive experiences she has facilitated. Her work in mediating sharing behavior is intentional. She asks, she probes, and she challenges students to see how sharing behavior benefits both their interpersonal relations and their shared academic successes.

Individuation

We live amid swarms of
people, yet there is a
vast distance between
people, a distance that
words cannot bridge.

—Richard Wright

In the United States, every newborn child receives a Social
Security number. This number is unique to the individual, different from all the other numbers that have been assigned.
When the individual has to deal with the government,
schools, banks, and businesses, he provides that special
number so that all his documents are coded solely to him.

The Social Security number is an official recognition of the uniqueness of each individual. It is that official uniqueness that identifies how each person is different from all others according to the records. The learning mediator fosters mediation by helping each student establish what it is that makes him a unique human being. Obviously, this task is more difficult and more important than merely assigning the individual a Social Security number.

■ The Mediation of Individuation

Mediation of individuation is the process of empowering each student to establish an internal locus of control. It is this locus of control which enables a person to take responsibility for his own life and to make decisions that chart his own direction. As the young child grows toward adulthood, the parent and teacher mediators lessen their control and help the child develop independent and original ways of thinking and acting. To accomplish this, the adult mediators acknowledge the differences between this child and the others with whom he works. Differences in style, intelligence, ability, past experience, and desire become the foundation for the mediator to encourage the child to chart his own path through life.

From the time the parent encourages the infant to stand and walk without support, throughout childhood and adolsecence, until the day the young adult elects to leave home, the mediation of individuation is a delicate task requiring balance and finesse. First, the parent mediator must respect the child's natural desire to be his own person without taking on completely a laissez faire approach. Second, the parent must encourage the child to take control of his behavior to the point that the child will not endanger himself or others. Third, the parent must respect the child's right to privacy while setting clear boundaries for all family members. Fourth, the parent must encourage the development of interests and abilities. without expecting the child to become a clone. Finally, the parent who wishes to develop that feeling of autonomy so critical to individuation must provide guidance in understanding the family's values and beliefs.

In the classroom the effective teacher/mediator must walk the same fine line. On the one hand the teacher/mediator must refrain from superimposing her own values and beliefs on the students; on the other hand it is important that the teacher/mediator helps students understand and respect the importance of family and community values. In the broadest sense this means that the teacher/mediator will have the most success with the mediation of individuation through a learner-centered approach. Students have a variety of interests, learning styles, levels of motivation, and cultural backgrounds. Today, more than ever, teachers must have a variety of ways to meet the

Mediation of individuation is the process of empowering each student to establish an internal locus of control.

needs of all the students in their classrooms. Whole class instruction (the "one size fits all" approach) has been the principal mode of instruction for decades. This method is decreasingly relevant. The students who are the most difficult to teach and the most challenging to motivate are among those we are least prepared to teach in a heterogeneous setting.

In a learner-centered classroom the teacher's chief concern is the development of self-directed learners. This long-range task is not easily accomplished. Just as growing up is a process of becoming an autonomous, responsible individual within the context of family values, becoming a self-directed learner is a process of becoming an autonomous, responsible learner within the context of community values. Young people will make wrong choices; they will make mistakes; they will also make correct choices and learn from their mistakes. It is the job of the mediator to help them learn from all their choices.

To help self-directed learners emerge from their dependence on the teacher, the teacher/mediator carefully considers the variety of students' needs, styles, and intelligences in building a curriculum that benefits all of the students assigned to the classroom. There are seven helpful guidelines to consider:

1. encourage each student to stand up for her beliefs;
2. motivate each student to develop her multiple intelligences;
3. give each student the tools to think critically about all points of view;
4. organize the celebration of cultural diversity;
5. welcome original ideas and creative thinking;
6. enhance the development of each child's special abilities; and
7. respect each child's values and beliefs.

In the urban classroom individuation takes on a special meaning. Today's student in the urban school comes under tremendous pressure to abandon family values and to adopt the values of the dominant gangs in the neighborhood. It is not too much to say that their very lives are at stake if they resist gang pressures. It is also not too much to assert that fear, confusion, and many other emotions dominate their thoughts in the classroom and create a major barrier to learning. Thus, the guidelines for learner-centered instruction have a double import in the urban school: the guidelines also point out why the process of learning must be at least an equal partner with the content of the curriculum.

Thus, it is most important that the mediator translate the guidelines into action. Howard Gardner's theory of the multiple intelligences provides one of the easiest and most beneficial frameworks for making the learner-centered guidelines useful in a classroom.

> The teacher's chief concern is the development of self-directed learners.

□ Multiple Intelligences

First, it is helpful to review the framework established by Gardner in his book *Frames of Mind* (1983). He wrote this book to challenge the popular notion that intelligence was a single intellectual capacity, of fixed ability, and measurable quantitatively. He declared at that time that intelligence was multiple in its capacities, changeable in its abilities, and assessable only in its multiplicity.

Gardner theorized that there are seven intelligences (in August 1995 he proposed an eighth, "the naturalist"). Relying on the accumulation of knowledge about the human brain and human cultures, Gardner has defined intelligence as "a human intellectual competence that entails a set of skills for problem solving—enabling the individual to resolve genuine problems or difficulties that he or she encounters and, when appropriate, to create an effective product" (1993). Furthermore, he describes an intelligence as "a biological and psychological potential; that potential is capable of being realized to a greater or lesser extent as a consequence of the experiential, cultural and motivational factors that affect a person" (Gardner 1995). At the same time that he was arguing for intelligence as a dynamic, changing, and active process that differed radically in different cultures, Gardner was rejecting both the popular notion that intelligence was a fixed capability resulting from an *a priori* definition and the factoring of test scores as taught by Binet and those who value "the bell curve."

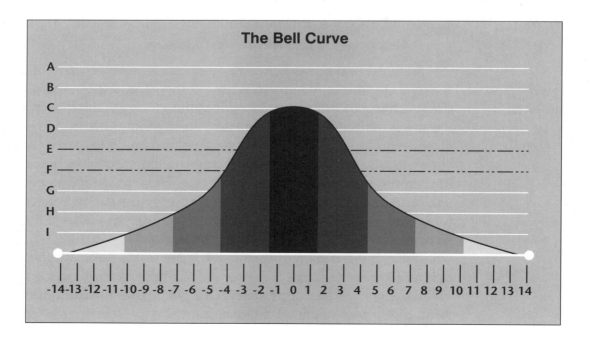

In order to establish an intelligence, Gardner developed eight stringent criteria. As his examination of how different cultures have solved problems would suggest a candidate "intelligence," he applied the criteria. When evidence showed that all eight criteria were met according to his standards, he named the intelligence. Using this approach, Gardner also has acknowledged that there is not a magical number of intelligences. To date, he has identified eight that meet all the criteria.

Criterion 1—Potential Isolation by Brain Damage

Gardner postulates that an intelligence is autonomous when it can be obliterated or preserved in isolation after trauma to the brain. For example, speech is a faculty that can be impaired or totally absent following a head injury, while other faculties survive unimpaired.

Criterion 2—The Existence of Prodigies, Mentally Handicapped Individuals with Savant Behaviors, and Other Exceptional Individuals

Although each individual presents a jagged profile of the multiple intelligences as unique as one's fingerprints, there are rare cases of what Gardner calls "highly uneven profiles of abilities and deficits." In these examples, again, the particular intelligences can be scrutinized discretely, in isolation. The super-occurrence or total absence of a faculty in itself suggests the very existence of that intelligence.

Criterion 3—An Identifiable Core Operation or Set of Operations

According to Gardner's work, it appears that an intelligence is sparked by certain kinds of stimuli inherent to the particular intelligence. For instance, the verbal/linguistic intelligence can be set in motion by the reading of a familiar line that in turn triggers the words remaining within that context (e.g., "'Twas the night before Christmas . . ." primes the pump, and one spews out ". . . and all through the house, not a creature was stirring, not even a mouse")—the core operation of the verbal/linguistic intelligence has thus been activated.

Criterion 4—A Distinctive Developmental History, along with a Definable Set of Expert "End-State" Performances

As illustrated throughout this text with the developmental path diagrams, each intelligence presents a traceable path toward proficiency—basic, complex, and higher order. Gardner also states that although all individuals pass through the various stages, only those with unusual talents may develop the highest level of expertise. For example, although we all experience the early awkwardness and eventual smoothness of figure skating, only the highly trained talent can execute the complex jumps and spins of the double and triple axel.

Criterion 5—An Evolutionary History and Evolutionary Plausibility

The idea that our existing intelligences link back to earlier species and to earlier forms of our species is also part of Gardner's thinking. He suggests that an intelligence becomes more plausible if it has some evolutionary roots that can be traced to today's phenomenon. A simple illustration is the early cave drawings and archeological artifacts and pottery that precede modern art in the area of visual/spatial intelligence.

Criterion 6—Support from Experimental Psychological Tasks

Demonstration of a particular intelligence seems to be a reasonable criterion, Gardner suggests, and often the demonstration is illuminated through the experiments of cognitive psychologists. For example, the ability to detect a logical pattern or visualize and solve a jigsaw puzzle are typical investigations of the logical/mathematical and visual/spatial intelligences.

Criterion 7—Support from Psychometric Findings

Along similar lines of psychological experimentation are the standardized tests that provide complementary evidence of the existence of an intelligence. Although Gardner cautions one to use these measures gingerly, he nevertheless includes this traditional criterion as yet another test of validity and reliability. If one performs well on an abstract reasoning problem, evidence of a logical/mathematical intelligence is more than merely implied—it becomes explicit.

Criterion 8—Susceptibility to Encoding in a Symbol System

Gardner's commonsense approach to what an intelligence is, is exemplified in this criterion, as he explains that what makes a particular intelligence useful to humans in problem solving and production is the ease with which it can be "exploited." For example, the fact that language and mathematics, graphic illustrations, dance, choreography, and musical notation can be encoded into universally understood symbols allows easy access and use of the intelligences.

■ The Eight Intelligences

Gardner is the first to admit that his list of multiple ways of problem solving and making products is not all encompassing. The current list identifies those eight intelligences which up until now have met *all eight criteria.* Continued study by Gardner, his colleagues, and others who accept the definition and the criteria may identify one or one hundred more intelligences.

1. Verbal/Linguistic Intelligence

I have to really feel a song before I'll deal with it and just about every song I do is based either on an experience I've had or an experience someone I knew had gone through.
—Aretha Franklin

The verbal/linguistic intelligence is concerned with the uses of language. People with this intelligence possess a particularly strong sensitivity to the meaning of words and a skilled aptitude with their manipulation. According to Gardner, these people have "the capacity to follow rules of grammar, and, on carefully selected occasions, to violate them" (Gardner 1983, 77). On yet another level—the sensory level—those with a heightened verbal/linguistic intelligence are able to communicate effectively by listening, speaking, reading, writing, and linking. They also have a strong awareness of the varying functions of language or, more specifically, its power to stimulate emotions. Poets, authors, reporters, speakers, attorneys, talk-show hosts, and politicians typically exhibit verbal/linguistic intelligence.

2. Musical/Rhythmic Intelligence

He who asks questions cannot avoid the answers.
—Cameroonian proverb

As Gardner describes it, "There are several roles that musically inclined individuals can assume ranging from the avant-garde composer who attempts to create a new idiom, to the fledgling listener who is trying to make sense of nursery rhymes (or other 'primer level' music)" (Gardner 1983, 104—5). Each of us holds musical capabilities to some degree—the difference is that some people have more skill than others. No matter what range of talent, we all possess a core of abilities necessary for enjoying a musical experience. These consist of the musical elements of pitch, rhythm, and timbre (the characteristic elements of a tone). People with more highly developed musical/rhythmic intelligence are singers, composers, instrumentalists, conductors, and those who enjoy, understand, or appreciate music.

3. Logical/Mathematical Intelligence

Our eyes see something; we take a stone and aim at it. But the stone rarely succeeds like the eye in hitting the mark.
—Nigerian proverb

The logical/mathematical intelligence incorporates both mathematical and scientific abilities. Mathematicians are typically characterized by a love of working with abstraction and a desire for exploration. They enjoy working with problems that require a great deal of reasoning. A scientist, however, is "motivated by a desire to explain physical reality"; for scientists, mathematics serves as a tool "for building models and theories that can describe and eventually explain the operation of the world" (Gardner 1983, 145). Mathematicians, engineers, physicists, astronomers, customer programmers, and researchers demonstrate a high degree of logical/mathematical intelligence.

4. Visual/Spatial Intelligence

Visual/spatial intelligence involves the unique ability to visually comprehend the world with accuracy. Those with visual/spatial intelligence are able to represent spatial information graphically and have a keen gift for bringing forth and transforming mental images. Artists and designers have strong visual/ spatial capabilities. They have a certain responsiveness to the visual/ spatial world, as well as a talent for recreating it in producing works of art. Sailors, engineers, surgeons, sculptors, cartographers, and architects are also notable for their strong visual/spatial intelligence.

5. Bodily/Kinesthetic Intelligence

The bodily/kinesthetic intelligence is the command of one's bodily motions and the talent to manipulate objects with deftness. It is possible for these abilities to exist separately, though most people possess both simultaneously. Those with keen bodily/kinesthetic intelligence include actors, dancers, acrobats, and athletes.

6. Intrapersonal Intelligence

The heart of intrapersonal intelligence lies in the ability to understand one's own feelings. People strong in this intelligence instinctively comprehend their own range of emotions, can label them, and can draw on them as a means of directing their own behavior. In Gardner's words "the intrapersonal intelligence amounts to little more than the capacity to distinguish a feeling of pleasure from one of pain, and on the basis of such discrimination, to become more involved in or to withdraw from a situation" (Gardner 1983, 239). Examples of those with higher-than-average intrapersonal capabilities include the introspective novelist, wise elder, psychologist, or therapist—all of whom possess a deep understanding of their feelings.

7. Interpersonal Intelligence

Intrapersonal intelligence is directed inward; interpersonal intelligence, though, is directed outward to others in the environment. The most basic skill among those with a high degree of interpersonal intelligence is the talent for understanding others. Those exhibiting this intelligence have the gift for noticing and making distinctions among other individuals, and more specifically among their "moods, temperaments, motivations, and intentions" (Gardner 1983, 239). For example, at a very simple level, this intelligence includes the ability of a child to notice and be sensitive to the moods of adults around him. A more complex interpersonal skill is that of adults being able to read the intentions of others, even when hidden. People typically exhibiting this intelligence include religious and political leaders, parents, teachers, therapists, and counselors.

8. Naturalist Intelligence

The naturalist is Gardner's most recently identified intelligence. A person with a strong naturalist intelligence is distinguished by the ability to understand, relate to, and function in the natural world. Linnaeus and Darwin are examples of individuals with a highly developed naturalist intelligence.

■ Criteria for Applying MI Theory

When Gardner first described the intelligences, he refrained from prescribing how to use his theory as instructional practice. After more than a decade of observation, he has developed criteria and a set of concerns to assist educators in making quality applications of his theory to the classroom.

First, let us consider the criteria that Gardner developed for assessing the quality application of his theory.

1. *Does the school curriculum cultivate multiple capabilities in students?* Gardner has often criticized schools for their overemphasis on the logical/mathematical and the verbal/linguistic intelligences in the curriculum. He advocates that schools develop curricula that allow for the equal development of student potential through the other intelligences. Thus, instead of regarding music and the visual arts as add-ons or extracurricular activities, schools with a solid application of his theory will restructure the curricula to allow as much instruction time for the fine arts as are allowed for reading, writing, and arithmetic.

2. *Does the school curriculum encourage the serious treatment of concepts, subject matter, and disciplines in a variety of ways?* Gardner advocates the "selective abandonment" (Art Costa's term) of trivial and outdated material in the curriculum so that teachers can provide in-depth treatment of significant key concepts and essential questions. Given less material "to cover," teachers can work more in-depth with a greater variety of approaches that are more appropriate pedagogically for targeted lessons or units. Thus, instead of listening to a teacher talk rapidly through content, students can engage in a variety of hands-on activities with time to explore, discuss, and experiment with the ideas.

3. *Does the school curriculum encourage the personalization of instruction?* Feuerstein's guidelines for empowering students through learner-centered instruction relate directly to Gardner's call for personalized classrooms in which curriculum, instruction, and assessment are built around individual needs in the classroom. Although uniform instruction may make teaching easier, regimented instruction's inability to benefit so many individuals, especially the diverse populations in urban schools, is well documented.

4. *Does the school curriculum encourage a variety of significant assessment approaches?* Although pen-and-pencil tests may make the grading of factual recall easier, it does little to show how well a student understands a topic, has mastered skills, or can demonstrate increased intellectual capability. Gardner advocates the selection of multiple means of assessment, each geared to show the range and depth of students' intellectual development. In his view tests that call for factual answers about the history of music or about the types of paint brushes used by Renoir may grade easily on the scantron, but they are inadequate for showing how well a student can play a new score or create a landscape of her own. In the multiple intelligence framework, the well-taught student not only will demonstrate how she has improved in these areas by playing the piece or completing the painting, she will have developed the ability to explain the importance of her accomplishment.

5. *Do curriculum, instruction, and assessment challenge students to develop their multiple intelligences?* The key word here is "challenge." As does Feuerstein, Gardner is concerned with the trivialization of his theory as a means to justify the continuation of trivial curricula, instruction, and assessment. In a multiple intelligences school, the system links the three tightly together in a significant way. However, in a school where assessment focuses on facts and isolated skills, instruction is low-level. Thus, when multiple intelligences practices are introduced into such low-level systems, the musical intelligence becomes mnemonics, the spatial intelligence becomes "dot-to-dot" pictures, and the verbal/linguistic intelligence becomes the memorization of vocabulary, spelling, and grammar rules by catchy songs. On the other hand, significant assessments that focus students on the understanding and application of ideas that Gardner calls for raises the level of curriculum and instruction. In this milieu multiple intelligences theory transforms key curricular ideas such as "democracy" into problem-based situations that challenge students to use different intelligences to understand the topic and to make applications relevant to their lives (Gardner 1995). Students don't give up learning how to read or write—they are asked to develop these basic skills in a real-world context but not as isolated or fragmented bits.

■ The Key School

The Key School in Indianapolis is one example of an urban school that has taken advantage of Gardner's theory to create a school that individuates instruction. Unlike "individualized instruction" which calls on the teacher to deliver a uniform curriculum with adaptations to each individual child, the individuated approach calls on the teacher to create learning situations which encourage each child to develop her unique talents.

The Key School is most definitely not a traditional school. Rewards and competition are not valued; grades are not given. Although there is a regular mandated curriculum in the main content areas common to most schools, an additonal curriculum of apprenticelike "pods"—which all students can choose according to their interests and abilities—is an integral part of the school's program. Through the pods, school staff work to strengthen students' talents and build upon their interests.

The school's population is drawn from the city of Indianapolis, and admission is based on lottery. Diversity is reflected in the fact that the school pulls a large percentage of minority children—45% at the elementary and middle school levels and 30% who qualify for free or reduced lunch.

Although the foundation of the school is cemented in years of teacher planning, research, and small seed grants, Principal Pat Bolanos explains that the multiple intelligences theory of Howard Gardner provided the theoretical framework upon which the school could be built. Gardner's theory of multiple intelligences resonated with the original eight teachers who decided to form the school, who found Gardner's ideas sympathetic to their own beliefs and educational philosophy.

■ The New City School

A second urban school, the New City School in St. Louis, has made a different application of Gardner's theories.

The New City School, an independent school with 355 students, admits students from the age of 3 through the sixth grade level. Drawing from forty-seven zip codes in the St. Louis area, the school has a 26% minority population and provides financial assistance to approximately 20% of its students. MI theory met with little resistance when its principal, Tom Hoerr, decided to explore its concepts with his staff.

In contrast to the Key School, the New City School tried pods and abandoned them, Hoerr says. "We imagine kids having seven different little test tubes—all of which need to be filled as much as possible. If you look at the American high school, it offers a multiple intelligences approach because it has drama club and art club and P.E. But by the time kids get to high school, the damage is often done. They may have a talent but they're not 'smart.' We're trying to back up and help them see their strengths before they reach high school."

■ The Marsh Elementary School

The Marsh Elementary School in Rockford, Illinois, led by Principal Cheryl Foltz, has a population of seven hundred students (12% Hispanic American, 25% African American, 63% Caucasian) and has used multiple intelligences theory to restructure curriculum, instruction, and assessment. In 1993, Principal Foltz and the faculty elected to join PDK/IRI's Multiple Intelligences Network (now the Network of Mindful Schools), a group of schools united by their belief in and practice of Gardner's theory. In the first year the network's coordinator introduced the faculty to Gardner's theory and practice. By 1996, grade level teams had introduced project-based learning, in which each project is designed to challenge and develop a variety of intelligences:

- instead of reading about how machines work and taking the traditional multiple-choice test, sixth-grade science students build a giant operating dragon which demonstrates the machine principles given in their textbook. Parents are involved in a dragon-building workshop so they can understand this learner-centered approach. In this project students develop all eight intelligences;
- in a first-grade classroom a "nature theme" leads to the building of bird houses, bee hives, and other "homes in nature." This project springs from the naturalist intelligence but also develops the verbal/linguistic, interpersonal, and logical/mathematical;
- in the eighth grade, a writer's club and a class newspaper project place basic skills into a real-world context. Although this project is primarily verbal/linguistic, students develop their visual/spatial, logical/mathematical, and interpersonal intelligences.

One of the strongest elements of this school's approach to instruction through the multiple intelligences is the development of alternative assessment and parent communication tools. In addition to the traditional assessments of basic skills via teacher-made tests and standardized achievement tests, every student has a colorful portfolio of work completed to share in parent conferences. Each season students perform for parents *in their classrooms*, present projects to their parents, and invite parents to special "Parents Learning, Too" nights. When parents arrive at the school, they are bombarded with student products that show evidence of the developing intelligences.

■ An Interdisciplinary Approach

One of the most successful ways for classroom teachers to use Gardner's theory as an individuation tool is to create interdisciplinary units that revolve around an important theme, concept, or question and allow students to select which intelligence they will use to anchor their study. For instance, note the multiple opportunities for studying the Constitutional Convention.

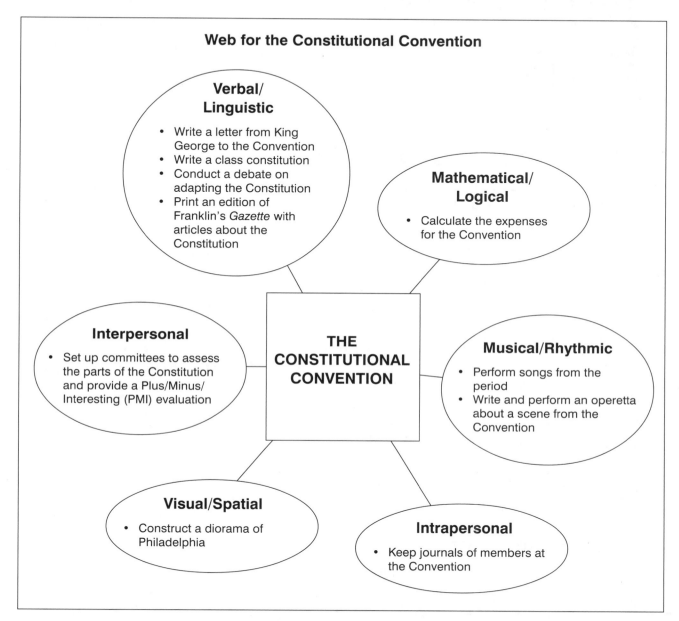

Web for the Constitutional Convention

Verbal/Linguistic
- Write a letter from King George to the Convention
- Write a class constitution
- Conduct a debate on adapting the Constitution
- Print an edition of Franklin's *Gazette* with articles about the Constitution

Mathematical/Logical
- Calculate the expenses for the Convention

Interpersonal
- Set up committees to assess the parts of the Constitution and provide a Plus/Minus/Interesting (PMI) evaluation

THE CONSTITUTIONAL CONVENTION

Musical/Rhythmic
- Perform songs from the period
- Write and perform an operetta about a scene from the Convention

Visual/Spatial
- Construct a diorama of Philadelphia

Intrapersonal
- Keep journals of members at the Convention

A second classroom approach allows for the creation of lessons which highlight several intelligences. In each of these sample lessons and the many others used throughout this book, students begin their study with a common problem. As they proceed through the lesson, each student receives ample opportunity to *individuate* work and to receive an individuated assessment. Pay special attention to how the final assessment checks each individual's understanding.

PRIMARY SCHOOL LESSON

Making Story Problems

Problem
How to write a story problem.

Focus Intelligences
Logical/Mathematical.

Supporting Intelligences
Visual/Spatial, Verbal/Linguistic.

■ CHECKING PRIOR KNOWLEDGE

1. On the board or overhead, create a sequence chart with eight to twelve blocks. Label the first and last blocks.

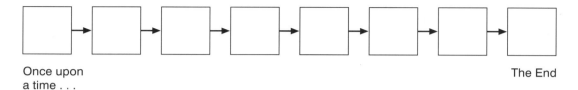

Once upon a time . . .   The End

2. Ask students to identify stories they have heard that begin "once upon a time . . ." List these on newsprint. After they have all contributed to the list, ask for a show of hands for those that have heard each story. Invite one youngster to share the story. (If students cannot identify one to tell, pick one or show a video such as "The Lion and the Mouse" or "How the Elephant Got His Trunk" (available from Encyclopaedia Britannica).

3. Chart the main events in the sequence chart for all to see and point out that all stories have events in a story that are arranged "start," "middle," and "end." Label these on the chart.

■ STRUCTURING THE TASK

1. Use the story you charted to introduce number problems. For instance, if you used the "Three Billy Goats Gruff," *(a)* the Three Billy Goats lived here (show picture), *(b)* all three crossed the bridge (show picture), or *(c)* no Billy Goats are here now (show picture). Next show numerical operation 3 – 3 = 0.

2. Invite a volunteer to tell you another story from the list or to invent a story. Chart the events on the board with sketches. Next, invite the class to add the number/word problem and complete the mathematics.

3. Practice additional examples each day. Select folk stories from a variety of cultures. Check for understanding of how to make a story problem:

    a. chart story with start, middle, and end;

    b. draw the story;

    c. write story with words and numbers;

    d. solve the problem;

    e. show example.

4. Form mixed groups of three. Assign roles (artist, storyteller, counter) and provide markers or crayons and paper. Review the process for creating a story problem for all to see.

5. Invite each group to make a new story problem. They may select any story not yet illustrated or invent a story to tell.

6. Work among the groups to mediate (a) how they make the story and (b) how they solve the problem.

7. Post the finished stories.

■ LOOKING BACK

Invite a member from each group to show the story problem and to point out how the group followed the process.

■ BRIDGING FORWARD

Introduce student journals so that *each student* can invent his or her own story problem. Encourage the group members to help each other. Work among the students to mediate their understandings. After stories are made, exchange them among the groups for solving. Mediate the thinking done to solve each problem. Collect each student's final work and individuate assessment by using the criteria below for each product.

Assessing Student Performance

To what degree can the student:

1. name the components of a story problem?

2. sequence the components in a logical order?

3. make a story problem using the components in a logical order?

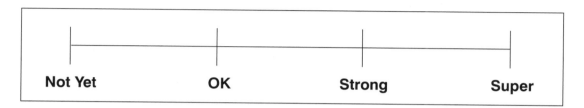

Not Yet   OK   Strong   Super

Materials

Newsprint, crayons, index cards, student journals.

Variations

1. Show different types of story problems and have groups learn to make each type.

2. Have students show their parents how to make a story problem and then bring to class a family-made example.

In a conventional classroom, mathematics is an isolated subject. Each topic and subtopic is isolated. Week by week, students work through each topic from addition, subtraction, multiplication, and division in the early grades to rational expressions, monomials, polynomials, and beyond in the secondary mathematics classroom (unless the students must repeat the basic computation until they "get it"!).

In the multiple intelligences classroom, which uses interdisciplinary projects, mathematics is integrated into projects that develop other intelligences simultaneously. Skills are not sequenced from simple to complex so that all students march forward (or stand still) in unison. In the context of the interdisciplinary unit, tasks requiring mathematical knowledge and skill are individuated. If a student must do mathematics and cannot, the teacher sets up a subgroup or individualized instruction mathematics module that fits the situation. If it is a complex mathematical task new to all in the project, the teacher uses the appropriate module with the entire class.

IRI/SkyLight Training and Publishing, Inc.

MIDDLE SCHOOL LESSON

Integrated Mathematics/ Language Arts

Publishing a Newspaper

Problem
How to publish a newspaper within a budget.

Focus Intelligence
Verbal/Linguistic.

Supporting Intelligences
Logical/Mathematical, Interpersonal, Visual/Spatial.

■ CHECKING PRIOR KNOWLEDGE

1. Students are grouped into trios. One student will record the group's ideas, one student will make sure all participate, and one will report the group's results.

2. On newsprint, each recorder will write out within six minutes (a) what the group knows/recalls about newspapers, (b) what the group's members hypothesize about newspaper productions, and (c) questions to ask.

3. After the know-hypothesize-question time is done, sample responses to each review item. Put the answers on the blackboard in three columns.

Know	Hypotheses	Questions

4. Add items that are left out by asking questions that challenge. Also, take time to discuss responses to the "Questions" column.

5. Let the class know that they are beginning a multiple month project to produce (you determine number) editions of a class newspaper.

■ STRUCTURING THE TASK

1. Use the trios to start research about the targeted audience for the paper (parents, students, other grades, community) and how other newspapers work with their own audiences:

   a. what is the paper's content going to be?

    b. what will the cost be?

    c. how will they market and sell the paper?

    d. who will gather the news?

    e. what budget will they need?

    f. who will have what responsibilities?

    g. what procedures will they follow in their jobs?

2. After jobs are assigned and costs determined, regroup students into departments (management, editorial, design, accounting, marketing, etc.). Each department will determine its budget. Make a master budget to show *(a)* all projected expenses, *(b)* anticipated income with sources, *(c)* gross profit after taxes (5–12%). You may wish to identify an accountant from parents or the community that can guide this process.

3. The best source of revenue will be ads. Involve the original groups of three in selling ads. They will turn these in to the business team with the collected funds. The business team may use a spreadsheet or database to keep the records, invoice, etc.

4. The trios will all write articles for the paper's first edition. The paper can include articles on class or student activities, current events, cartoons, sports news, community interviews, and surveys and editorials on "hot topics."

5. The trios will edit their own articles as well as those of other groups. After all articles and ads are finished, the design team will assemble the paper.

6. After distribution, the department teams will review budgets and calculate profit and loss. If a profit is generated, the teams can budget for a celebration.

■ LOOKING BACK

Conduct a five-minute reflection by asking each student to write down five things learned about producing a newspaper. Make random pairs in the class. Members of each pair will alternate for one minute each sharing one "I learned." After both have shared, each will select a new "I learned" and share it with the same partner for thirty seconds. After a third, fifteen-second alternate sharing, each will summarize what was learned in a wraparound.

■ BRIDGING FORWARD

Before each new edition, make a summary on the blackboard or posted on newsprint:

    a. what we did well in publishing this edition;

    b. what we want to do better in the next edition;

    c. help we need for a better edition.

IRI/SkyLight Training and Publishing, Inc.

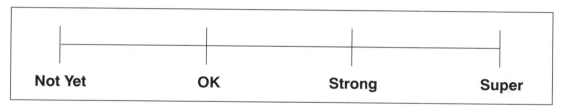

Assessing Student Performance

To what degree can each student:

| Not Yet | OK | Strong | Super |

1. identify the tasks for publishing a newspaper;
2. understand how to budget for a profit;
3. write a newspaper story using the 5 Ws;
4. sell and design ad copy;
5. collaborate with a team?

Materials

Sample newspapers for all students, budget outline sheets or computer software, graphic materials or computer software.

Variation

Set up any business that interests the students and has local resources: the bank, drug store, variety store, book publishing house, etc.

■ Multiple Intelligences and Content

In secondary classrooms which are content-dominated, another useful application of Gardner's theory is found in lessons which allow for the development of many intelligences without detracting from the core content. Indeed, the different intelligences enrich the unit or lesson and extend the possibilities for the mediation of individuation. In the advanced American history lesson below, note how the different intelligences are integrated as the means (1) for developing a deep understanding of each decade, (2) for mediating individuation, and (3) for promoting transference.

SECONDARY SCHOOL LESSON

Social Studies/ History

Problem
How to identify the distinguishing characteristics of a decade in American history.

Focus Intelligence
Interpersonal.

Supporting Intelligences
All.

■ CHECKING PRIOR KNOWLEDGE

Select a decade that you will use to model the process for identifying its distinguishing (define this word for students) characteristics. Divide the class into groups of three. Review roles and responsibilities of each group member (Recorder, Materials Manager, Leader). Assign each group one point of focus from this list: cultural, economic, artistic, military, political. Each group will use the dictionary to identify the meaning(s) of the assigned word, make a symbol for the word, and sketch pictures that represent the word. Regroup students into groups of five, one person having each word to teach to the others. After each word is shared with symbols, pictures, and explanations, the sharer will check for understanding among all group members.

■ STRUCTURING THE TASK

1. Reassemble the original trios. Use your combination of homework, reading, lecturette, video and/or group tasks for students to gather information about the decade. Each group will study the chapter with a focus on its assigned word (i.e., economic). The members will gather as much information on the assigned word for this decade as they can find. Once they have reviewed the information, they will create an advertisement that sells the specific benefits of that focus word in this decade.

2. Each group will do a poster presentation with its advertisement. After all presentations are completed, put an attribute web on the board with five rays. Mediate an all-class discussion, the purpose of which is to select the five characteristics of this decade which most make it unique:

   a. what are the characteristics you want to nominate? any others?

   b. explain why your choice should stay in the selected five; what other reasons?

3. After all are given, clarified, and explained, use a five-to-fist vote. Each student has one five-point, one four-point, one three-point, one two-point, and one one-point vote. Five is the vote for the most important characteristics. Every person will vote on each item on the list. If not using a point vote, the person

will show the fist which counts zero. Have two students count and one record each tally. Place and number the top five on the web.

■ LOOKING BACK

1. Give a quiz with one or two important facts related to each of the subtopics.
2. Ask each student to summarize in a journal entry what was learned about his group's subtopic and why this subtopic was important for the decade.
3. Invite each student to identify how the interpersonal intelligence was used in this lesson.

■ BRIDGING FORWARD

Review the steps for selecting the characteristics of a decade:

1. select focus for a decade;
2. understand focus concept;
3. use focus to study the information;
4. create poster;
5. make presentation;
6. select characteristics of decade.

Ask individuals to discuss how they might benefit from using these steps in the study of future decades. Facilitate individual action plans.

Variation

1. Provide original requirement materials such as literature, music, essays, and other artifacts from a decade.
2. Add final products such as video, drama, poem, etc., that capture the key characteristics of a decade.
3. Have each group select a single decade to study.

□ Individuating Assessment

In addition to lessons and projects which promote individuation through multiple intelligences theory, the teacher can mediate any given lesson by selecting end products which individuate the assessment of student learning:

1. a final exam that asks higher-order questions (verbal/linguistic);
2. a concept map of the project's key ideas (visual/spatial);
3. sample mathematical problems requiring solution that test problem-solving abilities (logical/mathematical);

4. self-assessment that demonstrates the ability to perform a learned task according to a set of criteria (intrapersonal);

5. a written essay on the content of the project (verbal/linguistic).

Finally, individuation comes down to the questions that a mediator poses to an individual student. Through this questioning process, the mediator can mediate individuation by connecting the student's intelligences to the classroom discussion. In this way the teacher helps each student develop her best ways to think and to act:

- "If you were to express this idea in a short story, what would be the conflict?" (verbal/linguistic)
- "If you were to express this idea as a symbol, what would it look like?" (visual/spatial)
- "Explain this idea as a math formula." (logical/mathematical)
- "Where would I find examples of this concept in the natural world?" (naturalist)
- "How might a musician express that?" (musical/rhythmic)
- "How does this idea affect your life?" (intrapersonal)
- "How could this idea help us get along better?" (interpersonal)
- "Show me how to express the idea through mime." (bodily/ kinesthetic)

☐ Conclusion

Multiple intelligences theory and practice is an especially helpful framework for the mediation of each child's thinking. Individuation gives the mediator a rich opportunity to help students move through the developmental stages that lead to independent thinking and acting in a purposeful and constructive way.

IRI/SkyLight Training and Publishing, Inc.

Goal Planning

Indecision is like the
stepchild: if he doesn't
wash his hands, he is
called dirty; if he does,
he is wasting water.

—Madagascan proverb

In a high-tech society where instant gratification is the norm, many young people do not stop to think of planning their time, developing goals, or looking to the future. From TV they learn that it is easier to grab the moment or to steal what they like, rip-off a professional sports jacket or a high-priced pair of shoes, drive by homes and shoot gang rivals or inno- cent children, paint empty walls with graffiti signatures and gang signs, snort cocaine or smoke marijuana, hang out at the mall or on the corner. Impulsive behavior is more fun.

◘ The Mediation of Goal Planning

When students live in an instant gratification culture, especially when they are bombarded with images of wealth that they lack, the mediation of goal planning becomes a critical tool for countering impulsive behavior. Mediation of goal planning occurs when the teacher guides and directs the student through the processes involved in setting and planning strategies and in achieving short- and long-term goals. The mediator increases the effectiveness of the process by making it explicit so that the student can take responsibility for charting her own accomplishments in achieving the goals.

The mediation of goal planning becomes a critical tool for countering impulsive behavior.

As with other interactions that promote behavior control and reduce impulsive actions, the most effective goal planning occurs when it is connected to academic achievement. For students alienated from academics, though, the mediator may still use goal planning successfully to delay gratification and to control impulsive behavior. (In this regard, the mediation of goal planning is connected to the mediation of competence, regulation of behavior, individuation, challenge, and self-change.) The mediator will understand that the greater the impulsivity of a student or class, the greater the need to mediate goal planning.

◘ Four Aspects of Goal Setting

In mediating goal planning it is helpful for the mediator to start with an explicit introduction of the process, with material the students are familiar with or with non-serious material that does not distract the students from the goal setting process. To introduce the process, the teacher can prepare a bulletin board or handout that details the three criteria for goal setting as they are embodied in a four-aspect plan for carrying out the process:

1. Set a target that is realistic and appropriate and discuss how it meets the ABC criteria:

   A = *Achievable.* Does the student see the goal as possible to reach given her talents and limits?

   B = *Believable.* Has the student seen a similar goal accomplished by someone like her?

   C = *Conceivable.* Can the student understand what it will take to achieve the goal?

2. Develop a step-by-step action plan to achieve the goal.

3. Evaluate the process used.

4. Finally, evaluate the result and make needed adjustments.

IRI/SkyLight Training and Publishing, Inc.

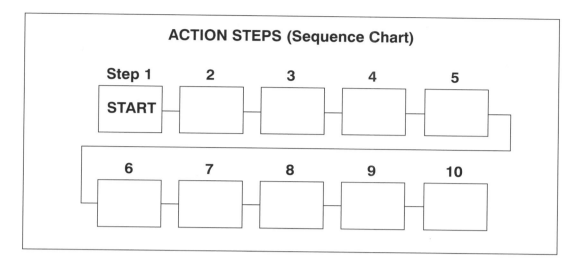

Using an academic lesson that the students have already mastered, the mediator will illustrate how to use the four aspects of goal setting. First, on the board she will write and label the goal. For instance, if the students have learned how to balance an algebraic equation, she will designate that as the goal and then label the goal statement. Next, she will list on the board the procedures or steps for balancing an equation and label these as aspect 2, the "step-by-step action plan." Third, she will work a sample problem and point out how she is performing each step as she does it. Finally, she will check to see if the solution is correct and label this as aspect 4. When the modeling is complete, the mediator will check for the students' understanding of the goal setting process before applying the same procedure to new content.

From this point forward, each time the teacher introduces new material, she will start with a review of the four aspects by asking students to explain each aspect and give examples from their experience. During the lesson she will ask different students to label and explain the goal setting aspects as they occur (and here is a good opportunity to use the TESA skills). At the end of the lesson or unit, she can use a variety of assessment strategies that engage the students in evaluating their content mastery and their use of the goal setting process.

■ The Rubric: Standards and Criteria

As the teacher sets goals for activities, lessons, or units with the class, she can reinforce the goal setting behavior by sharing with the students the rubric by which she will assess their work. The rubric outlines the standards and criteria that will enable the students and the teacher to assess the quality of their work. When coupled with curriculum content, framed either by applications of Gardner's multiple intelligences theory or by transfer-of-thinking strategies learned from Feuerstein's Instrumental Enrichment, the rubric creates a road map for students and teacher alike. Instead of allowing students to sit passively in the classroom without holding the teacher accountable or the student responsible, the rubric announces early on the performance expectations for everyone and reinforces the goal planning process.

First, the mediator selects a standard and discusses it with the students. The mediator points out that this is not a lesson in which the class will simply cover certain material, as for instance "Today we will read Chapter 13—The Age of Discovery," or "Today we will discuss Chapter 5—Understanding Fractions," or "This week we're going to read and discuss *Hamlet*." Instead, the mediator will discuss with the class what abilities or understandings they will develop during this unit of study. For instance, if the content standard states that as a result of activities in the unit, all students will develop the abilities to perform scientific inquiry (National Standards, Science Education, 1994 draft), she will explain and give an example of scientific inquiry. Second, the mediator will list what the students will learn and then review the criteria for the levels of performance she will expect. For instance, the unit in scientific inquiry will show each student how to plan and conduct a simple investigation, use simple equipment to gather data, use the data to construct an explanation, and communicate the results.

The finished rubric, posted in the classroom, will look like this:

Rubric

Standard

You will show me that you can *perform* a scientific inquiry.

Content

You will learn how to do the following:

1. plan and complete a project that shows how energy flows;
2. use water beakers and other tools to gather data on your project;
3. explain with a labeled drawing the data you accumulated;
4. make a presentation to the class about what you discovered.

Performance Criteria

You and I will decide on the pluses and minuses of four products: your plan, your use of the tools, your drawing, and your presentation. We will use the scales shown below. After you mark each one, think about what data you have to back up your assessment.

Continued on next page

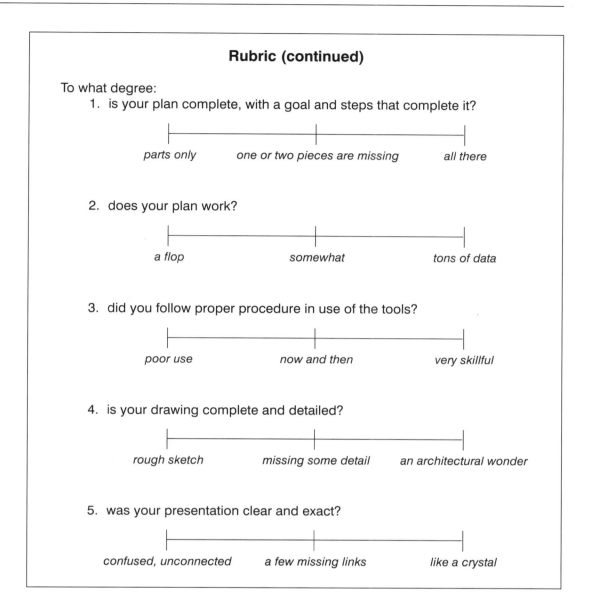

Rubric (continued)

To what degree:

1. is your plan complete, with a goal and steps that complete it?

parts only	one or two pieces are missing	all there

2. does your plan work?

a flop	somewhat	tons of data

3. did you follow proper procedure in use of the tools?

poor use	now and then	very skillful

4. is your drawing complete and detailed?

rough sketch	missing some detail	an architectural wonder

5. was your presentation clear and exact?

confused, unconnected	a few missing links	like a crystal

After the mediator has reviewed the posted rubric, she has the option of providing samples of student work from previous years to illustrate the levels of performance. Finally, before she starts the unit itself, she will convene a goal setting session. A simple form for inclusion in students' portfolios, to use as a journal entry or to turn in for review by the teacher, will suffice.

Goal Setting

Name _____

Class_____ Date _____

Unit Title: Energy

My goals:

   1.

   2.

   3.

   4.

How I will carry out these goals:

   1.

   2.

   3.

   4.

Although it might benefit students for the teacher to mediate goal setting before every single lesson, it is most likely that time will not permit such coverage without a major abandonment of content in the curriculum. However, when starting new units of study, there is good evidence to support the use of time in introducing the goal setting process at a unit's start and to revisit it through mediation as students work through and complete the project.

In the course of the project, the mediator may use such goal planning interventions as:

- Let's review the process.
- How does this step fit with your goal?
- What progress are you making toward the goal?
- Are there any steps you need to change?
- Are you running into any obstacles you didn't anticipate?
- Let's review our progress and redefine our aims.

❑ Reflective Goal-Setting Strategies

At the end of the project, the mediator can ask the students to assess both the process used, the final products and what content the students learned.

IRI/SkyLight Training and Publishing, Inc.

This works best when the students take time to think or write in their journals before talking the project over. Here are some reflective strategies:

The 3-2-1 Goal Planning Review

Direct students to form pairs. Each pair will have three minutes to review the goal setting process as it was used in the unit just completed. Next, give the pairs two minutes to discuss what they learned from the experience about planning. Finally, each pair will develop in one minute a key question to ask the class about the completed goal planning. Write three to five questions on the board and spend three minutes sharing answers for each.

Five Minute Think-Pair-Share

Give each student two minutes to *think* about and write down five things he learned about the goal planning process in this unit. Next, *pair* the students and have each pair *share* their respective lists (allow one minute each). Partners should not repeat ideas heard from their partners. Continue the alternate talk for another thirty seconds each. Do a third alternate talk with no repeats for fifteen seconds each. (Adapt this strategy to products or to content.)

Goal Processing Wraparound

Give the students thirty to sixty seconds to think about and complete one of these stems:

> About goal planning I learned. . . .
> In this lesson I improved my goal planning by. . . .
> In this lesson the aspect of goal planning that I performed best was. . . .

Goal Planning PMI

Present each student with a PMI chart. Ask each to note what the pluses were about his goal planning in this unit; repeat the notations for the minuses (column 2) and interesting questions (column 3).

P	
M	
I	

Three Questions for Reflection

Ask each student to think about or write about in a journal the goal planning used in this unit:

1. What was important about the goal planning you just completed?
2. How can you apply goal planning to other school tasks?
3. What steps will you take to use goal planning with another school task?

☐ Goal-Planning Activities

Beyond these short verbal mediation strategies, there are a variety of goal-planning activities which will help students develop these skills, enabling them to understand and appreciate this process. These strategies work best when they are embedded in lessons which provide hands-on activities and assessment.

Goal-Setting Activity—Score

Problem
How to set reachable goals.

Focus Intelligence
Bodily/Kinesthetic.

Supporting Intelligences
Interpersonal, Intrapersonal.

■ CHECKING PRIOR KNOWLEDGE

Young students see many games on TV—basketball, hockey, football. They know that the object of most games is to score high. Baskets, goals, and touchdowns are common terms to them. Ask the class to brainstorm all the sports in which scoring points is important. List the sport and the way a player gets points (e.g., touchdown).

■ STRUCTURING THE TASK

1. Explain the connection between a goal in a game (e.g., touchdown, basket) and a goal in life (something we want).

2. Place a wastebasket on a chair. On the floor in front of the basket, mark two-foot lines with the scores.

3. Divide the class into four teams. Each team will have three minutes to get the highest score it can. All members must have a chance to shoot from one of the numbered squares.

4. Give each team three minutes to agree on a strategy. Points are scored by a "basket" x the box total (so, one shot scored from 4 = 4; five shots from 3 = 15). Have a box of crumpled 8 ½" x 11" paper ready for each round.

5. Total points on the board after each round for each team. Highest total wins.

■ LOOKING BACK

Ask each team to explain and judge its strategy in relation to its goal. Discuss what they would do differently the next time.

■ BRIDGING FORWARD

Each team will discuss and share this idea: "Scoring points in this game is like goal setting in life because _____ ."

Materials

Wastebasket, crumpled paper, chalk.

IRI/SkyLight Training and Publishing, Inc.

Variation

Each day for the next two weeks, allow the same teams to improve on their previous day's performance. Give three minutes to plan strategy beforehand and three minutes to evaluate after. At the end of the week, ask teams to explain in their own words the difference between a "strategy" and a "goal."

MIDDLE SCHOOL LESSON

Mapping a Plan

Problem
How to make a plan.

Focus Intelligence
Visual/Spatial.

Supporting Intelligences
Interpersonal, Intrapersonal, Verbal/Linguistic.

■ CHECKING PRIOR KNOWLEDGE

Divide the class into pairs. Give each pair a large sheet of paper and a marker. On the board or overhead list these situations:

1. reaching the Moon
2. finding the Wizard of Oz
3. discovering Atlantis
4. traveling to the Antarctic
5. visiting grandmother's house.

Ask students to identify the common elements in each (someone taking a trip, going someplace, having a goal based on a story, etc.). After you have discussed the items, tell each pair to select one as a basis for a planning task they will complete together.

■ STRUCTURING THE TASK

1. Identify and define each of the following words:

   Goal: a desired state or place

   Pitfall: a trap

   Barrier: a block or obstacle

2. On the paper, each pair will sketch its starting point and its goal. (Model on the overhead or board.)

           * The Goal

   * The Start

3. They will sketch at least three alternate paths from the start to the goal. Each path will have at least three different pitfalls or barriers. They should sketch these in place. No words are to be used.

4. They will sketch in a picture of the means by which they propose to avoid the pitfalls and bypass the barriers.

■ LOOKING BACK

After you have joined pairs into fours, instruct the pairs to use the ABC interview sheet (see "The ABCs of Scoring Goals," p. 165). Each pair will be on focus for eight minutes to describe its chart and the thinking used to make decisions and to respond to the ABC interview.

■ BRIDGING FORWARD

Introduce these two stems:

> About goal planning—
>
>> An idea I can use in other classes . . .
>>
>> I wonder what will happen when . . .

Use an all-class wraparound to hear the responses.

IRI/SkyLight Training and Publishing, Inc.

The ABCs of Scoring Goals

Problem
How to evaluate goals.

Focus Intelligence
Visual/Spatial.

Supporting Intelligences
Verbal/Linguistic, Interpersonal, Intrapersonal.

■ CHECKING PRIOR KNOWLEDGE

Ask students to define the word *goal* as they know it, and list synonyms (desires, wishes, wants, etc.) and types of goals (career, educational, personal, etc.) that they have. Then have them fill in a copy of this chart in their logs:

Goals		
Meaning	**Synonyms**	**Types**

■ STRUCTURING THE TASK

1. Share this information with a jigsaw:

   Realistic problem solving begins with the ABCs of goal setting: A = achievable, B = believable, and C = conceivable. These three criteria that can help students measure the quality of their goals. Consider each of these criteria.

   First, *Achievable:* An achievable goal is one that the individual can trace, step by step, from her current place to the actual attainment. This means that the goal is clear and explicit. On the long climb to the goal, the individual knows each step in sequence, which steps are critical, and which steps may need some adjusting. For instance, Sue, an outstanding fifteen-year-old tennis player, wants to reach her goal of playing professional tennis. She has thought carefully about what she must do. She knows, for instance, that she might practice a minimum of four hours per day, continue her weight program, control her diet as prescribed by a nutritionist, strengthen her serve, and so on. By breaking her long-term goal into manageable sequenced steps, she makes her goal more achievable.

Second, *Believable:* A believable goal is one that is built on a careful assess-ment of what is within one's grasp. Each of us will refine our vision of what is possible to us by our experience. Direct experience can be the best teacher; indirect experience also helps. For instance, Sue's mother may not find her goal of a career in professional tennis to be very believable because the mother has neither known of nor heard about an 'ordinary' young woman becoming a pro tennis player; the dream is virtually unbelievable. Sue and her mother both need concrete models. For Sue's mother there are none. Sue, however, has read about women pros in *Sports Illustrated,* has seen women's tennis at Wimbledon, has attended a local tournament, has a Steffi Graf autograph, and has interviewed her next-door neighbor, a pro women's coach, for the high school magazine. Sue's first-hand contact with women pros makes her goal believable.

Third, *Conceivable:* A conceivable goal is one built on solid assessment of one's strengths and weaknesses. The assessment is solid to the degree that one has good evidence from reliable sources of what one can and cannot do. Sue's coach is a reliable source. Weekly, she reviews a videotape of Sue's practice. Together, they keep a tally of how well Sue does with each different type of shot. They measure strength, accuracy, and attention. They can compare Sue's skills to others in her ability class, as well as to women pros, to evaluate her capability.

The ABCs of goal setting will help students clarify their goals and make them more realistic. When taken together, the ABCs help the students form a more realistic, picture of what is desired and the best means to that goal. By learning to use the ABC approach, the students will give themselves a tool that will set a very positive and clarifying framework for substantive problem solving.

2. Divide the students into groups of three. Assign numbers one, two, and three to the students in each group.

3. Introduce the words "clarify," "extend," "focus," and "support" by writing them on the board or overhead. Solicit several explanations and examples of each word. Instruct students to add the words to their vocabulary lists in the notes.

4. The person assigned the number one is the focus person. The other two in the group will focus their complete attention on the focus person for six minutes. After the focus person has had no more than three minutes to describe his goal with no interruptions from the others, they will ask goal-clarifying questions and extending questions to draw out the focus person. In no way will they argue with the focus person. They will use good eye contact, positive body language, and give nonverbal support to that person's responses. They will alternate questions for the final three minutes.

5. The focus person may select one of the following areas to share with his group:

   a. a career goal

   b. a skill goal

    c. an academic goal

    d. a product goal

    e. a task goal

    f. a personal relationship goal

    g. a personal improvement goal

    h. a family goal

    i. a spiritual goal

    j. a physical goal

    k. a travel goal.

The focus person will describe the goal as specifically as possible in the three minutes. One member will keep time. The focus person may wish to describe the reasons for the goal, the advantages, how it was selected, what benefits it might bring, the hardships that it presents, and so on.

6. After listening for three minutes maximum, the others in the group will alternate with questions using the ABC approach. All questions must come from this area unless it is necessary for the listeners to ask a clarifying question such as "Can you be more specific?" or "Can you give us an example?" ("Why?" and "Do you think . . .?" questions are out of bounds).

7. Conduct a model interview. Select a goal from your life and share it with the class. Have a timekeeper stop you after three minutes. Invite students to select questions from the list for you to answer. Do not forget the pass rule. In fact, this is a good chance to model that it is okay to say "I pass." After three or four questions check for understanding by asking for thumbs up, etc. On the instructions for the focus interview, clarify as needed and put the groups to work for the first round.

8. At the end of the time, instruct the focus person to give a specific "I appreciate . . ." to each partner for the assistance provided and to write into his log the original goal statement or any change made because of the clarification and support.

9. While the first focus person is completing a log entry, the others may prepare their goal statements. When you signal, the next person in the group will become the focus person. Complete this round as the first. When the second log entry is done, the third person will move to the focus and complete the round.

■ LOOKING BACK

Using a classroom wraparound, ask students in turn to respond to your processing lead-in: "From this goal-clarifying activity, I learned . . . ." Encourage all to listen carefully to the ideas. Ask volunteers to identify the similarities among the ideas heard. Have a student list these on paper or the blackboard. When several are listed, seek multiple responses to the following questions: "What conclusions can you draw from this list of similarities? Why? What general statements can you make about the worth or value of asking goal-clarifying questions? What might be some appropriate times or situations for you to ask yourself goal clarifying questions?"

■ BRIDGING FORWARD

Instruct students to use their logs. They might pick a different goal from the one first discussed in their groups. In their logs, have them write down one appropriate question they might ask themselves in each of the three ABC areas for that goal.

Students are often encouraged to set goals. There are multiple models around them that show the benefits of goal setting. Athletes set goals to win tournaments, super bowls, and championships. Auto manufacturers set sales goals. Nations set goals to end wars and advance peace. Whenever local personalities or national figures talk about "goals," it is helpful for the mediator to call these instances to the students' attention. Furthermore, it helps students internalize the process when they are asked how they have used the goal setting process in their daily academic work, how they have benefited from the goal setting process, and how the process is best used. Such mediation helps students transcend the specific goals so that they value process itself.

Challenge

When someone is taught
the joy of learning, it
becomes a lifelong
process that never stops,
a process that creates a
logical individual. That is
the challenge and joy of
teaching.

—Marva Collins

Researchers who try to understand what makes an effective
teacher seldom seem to follow Marva Collins's advice about
the joy of learning. Instead, they seem devoted to the behaviorist model and hold instead that the effective teacher has a
pocketful of motivational tricks and techniques, the effectiveness of which can be easily measured. According to author
Alfie Kohn, these techniques fall into two categories: rewards
and punishments. Rewards are good grades, gold stars,
praise, and warm fuzzies; punishments are low grades, criticism, time out or detention, and the forbidding "call home."

Kohn, Feuerstein, and Herzberg build on the tradition that prefers intrinsic motivation. In the mediation of challenge, the next criterion of mediating interactions, the mediator creates conditions and opportunities for students to achieve. These opportunities allow for the development of intrinsic motivation for completion of tasks which evoke feelings of interest, excitement, and determination, even though tasks may appear difficult. With support, encouragement, and mediation for challenge, students discover potentials previously unknown.

☐ The Mediation of Challenge

In the mediation of challenge, the mediator creates conditions and opportunities for students to achieve.

Consider students in two different elementary mathematics classrooms. In one the teacher hands out a worksheet with fifty-four number problems. She tells the students what to do and then sits down at her desk. If a student has a question, he lines up to the right of the teacher's desk and waits his turn. In the other classroom the teacher sits her students in groups of three. She gives each group a cup of dry corn and a cup of marbles. She asks each group to take out three pieces of corn and four marbles from the cups. The group has to agree quickly on the number of "pieces" they have. She repeats the process several times. Each time the problem becomes more difficult. The children become more excited with each new challenge. When all the corn and marbles are on the tables, she asks them to explain what they learned about adding the pieces. After their talk she gives them the first numbers to add. Once again, as they succeed, she ups the ante with a more difficult problem.

When a teacher or parent mediates challenge as in the second example, the students experience in their academics what novice skiers experience on the mountainside. First, there is the tension of the bunny hill. After the instructor coaches the skiers down the hill without a fall or picks up and restarts those who do fall, the novices return to the course on their own. As their confidence grows, the skiers tire: gone is the novelty of the initial challenge. Now they are sure and ready for the green runs. Once these are mastered, the skiers are ready for the tougher blue runs and, ultimately, for the double black diamond run. Do these students receive stickers and stars for each new triumph? No—their reward is the internal excitement and pleasure that comes with conquering fears, taking risks, and pushing one's limits.

Creating Challenges

What does the mediator do to create the challenges? First, she models an open and excited attitude about taking on the tougher word problem. As the student's body language and oral expression say "Oh my gosh, I will never do that," the mediator encourages, "I know this is tough, but I also know what you can do. Together we can do this."

Second, the mediator prepares a sequence of increasingly challenging and complex tasks. She charts the way for the students and shows them how they will conquer the "bunny hill" to get ready for the tougher runs. And she gives them a novel perspective: instead of the boring, repetitive worksheets that get "done" and filed, the mediator provides hands-on, activity-based situations that grow in difficulty, which the students see they will be able to conquer one at a time while their confidence grows.

Third, the mediator encourages creativity, curiosity, and originality in performing the tasks. As students master the basic steps, she provides more difficult tasks, and she challenges the students to figure new ways to solve the problem: "Tell me another idea you have"; "What's a different way?" The students try out their methods in search of the best approach.

Fourth, the mediator encourages appropriate risk taking. She pushes the students to use new approaches in the strategies that they want to try. "Will this stretch you? Will this take you out of your comfort zone?"

Fifth, the mediator helps students reflect on the reasons for their successes, identify their best work strategies, and build patterns of thinking into their methods. The mediator communicates her observations of their work with enthusiasm and excitement about her satisfaction with their progress. She places special emphasis on what they have chosen to do and what they have accomplished: "You picked this strategy; you made it work."

Three Things Not to Do

What a parent or teacher does *not* do may be as important as what he or she does do to mediate challenge. First, the mediator does not rescue students by interfering with or performing the task or answering the question. A mediator who steps in too soon without good wait time and takes over the task is denying students the necessary practice and the opportunity to correct mistakes.

Second, the mediator avoids using extrinsic behavior modification, especially with conditional promises of rewards: "If you do this, then I will give you . . . ." Conditional rewards build a student's dependency on the reward. As the student is satisfied with a small reward, the expectation of a bigger reward soon follows: first, the new pair of shoes; next, an expensive dress—how long before the car keys? Once caught in the extrinsic reward trap, the student loses focus on the fact that she had positive feelings about overcoming an obstacle that she had approached with uncertainty.

Third, the mediator avoids making the task seem insurmountable. Using the ski analogy, the mediator doesn't take the novice to the tip of the

What a parent or teacher does not do may be as important as what he or she does do to mediate challenge.

black diamond slope and say, "Ski down, I know you can do it." Risk that appears overwhelming is only discouraging.

■ Integrating Thinking across the Curriculum

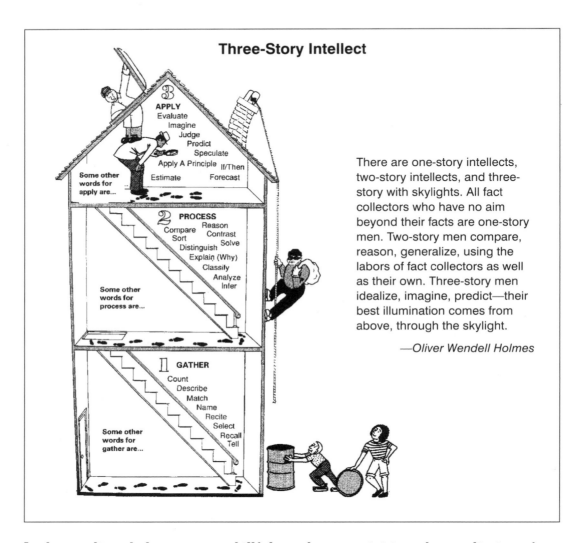

Three-Story Intellect

APPLY
Evaluate
Imagine
Judge
Predict
Speculate
Apply A Principle   If/Then
Estimate   Forecast

Some other words for apply are...

PROCESS
Compare   Reason
Sort   Contrast
Distinguish   Solve
Explain (Why)
Classify
Analyze
Infer

Some other words for process are...

GATHER
Count
Describe
Match
Name
Recite
Select
Recall
Tell

Some other words for gather are...

There are one-story intellects, two-story intellects, and three-story with skylights. All fact collectors who have no aim beyond their facts are one-story men. Two-story men compare, reason, generalize, using the labors of fact collectors as well as their own. Three-story men idealize, imagine, predict—their best illumination comes from above, through the skylight.

—*Oliver Wendell Holmes*

In the mediated classroom a skillful teacher may initiate the mediation of challenge by asking increasingly difficult question. "The Three-Story Intellect" provides one approach.

At first glance, this model appears to be a mere simplification of Bloom's taxonomy. However, unlike Bloom's monumental list which so many teachers, ironically enough, were asked to memorize, the three-story model is a useful tool for providing teachers with a challenging framework for increasing the challenge level of their mediational questions. All of the thinking skills detailed at each story were selected because of their regular and implicit use in the standard curriculum. For instance, it is a rare fourth-grade reading curriculum that does not ask students to begin making inferences, a "second story" skill that is essential for reading comprehension. In algebra, introduced to most students in the ninth grade, students are called upon to learn about logic. In quality high school composition programs, it is a regular practice to expect students to write essays that compare and contrast characters, genres, and thematic treatments and to forecast story endings.

Using the Three-Story Intellect Model

In the challenge classroom the teacher can use the three-story intellect model to stretch how students interact with the content in three ways. First, the model can be used to ask increasingly difficult questions in a discussion of the content. The teacher can check for understanding of the material by asking first-story questions, followed by second- and third-story questions:

1. *Name* the country with the largest land area in _____.
2. *Compare* the exports of that country to the exports of _____.
3. *Predict* the impact on world trade if this country's exports were closed to U.S. buyers.

Second, a teacher can mediate challenge by using the three-story model to restructure her curriculum. There are two elements used for restructuring a curriculum: content and process. For each of these, the restructuring starts with the realignment of goals (cf. goal planning). In current practice much of what happens in many classrooms is coverage of the textbook and completion of workbooks. In the question-centered classroom, the center of attention is given to deepening the student's understanding of the key concepts in a course.

To bring concepts into focus, the teacher who wants to mediate challenge will begin with the question: "When students finish this course, what will they know and be able to do?" After she has answered this question, she will ask, "What resources do I have that will help students accomplish the key concepts and skills?" From the text and other materials, she will select the supporting resources.

In a challenge classroom the text provides the students with a major resource, not chapters to cover. The teacher will select the chapters and pages that will most help with answering her questions. For the material she selects from the text, she will ask, "How will this material help the students achieve the objectives?" By implication her choices will retain the most important information and throw out the unrelated or extraneous material.

This selection process, called "selective abandonment," is one that most teacher candidates "cover" in their undergraduate preparation; unfortunately, they receive little practice in the art of selective abandonment. When

In the question-centered classroom, the center of attention is the student's understanding of key concepts in a course.

they take their first jobs, the system gives little or no support to concept-based instruction. Immediately, the textbooks and workbooks become the unselective guides that the novice must learn to cover chapter by chapter in thirty-six weeks. Indeed, the definition of "cover" as "to conceal" becomes a reality!

Take for instance a first-year teacher in a ninth-grade English class. On the first day of inservice in her career, she listens to a motivational speaker, attends a departmental meeting where she is handed her temporary list of students, the texts she will use, and her classroom number. The text looks familiar—it's the same one she used as a high school student. That night, she goes home and opens her lesson plan book next to the text. In the plan

M	T	W	Th	F
Roll Texts Rules	Read Anglo-Saxon History	Read *Beowulf*	Slides and *Beowulf* discussion	Test

book, she jots down what she will do the first week: "Monday: take roll and hand out texts; review classroom rules. Tuesday: read about the Anglo-Saxon period; Beowulf. Wednesday: Anglo-Saxon slide show. Thursday: Beowulf. Friday: Beowulf test." To prepare for the class lectures, she pulls out the notes from her college survey course, "English Literature 101."

How different it would be if she took the knowledge that she gained about literature and asked herself the question, "At the end of this course, what will the students know and be able to do?" Part of her answer might look like this: "My students will understand how great literature can inform our lives and help us make more thoughtful decisions in challenging situations" or "My students will be able to write a coherent three paragraph essay explaining how the literature they read informed their lives." With these answers in mind, how much easier and productive it would be to restructure the first and subsequent weeks: "Monday: take roll and ask students how literature may have informed their lives; give an example and use TESA behaviors to engage all; state expectations for course related to this discussion. Tuesday: introduce any writing expectations in a daily journal entry—each will react to literature read before we hold a classroom discussion. Tie their reflections to how literature informs our lives. Read and discuss Dr. King's 'Letter from the Birmingham Jail' as it relates to their past knowledge and experience. Journal entry—'What meaning does this letter have for us?'

M	Roll and Expectations Ask: How does literature inform our lives?
T	Journals: Reflections on Literature
W	King's letter: How does it inform our lives?
Th	Compare *Beowulf* and King's letter New journal reflections
F	Writing lesson: Use Venn diagram to compare the two works with our lives.

Wednesday: discuss journal entry and provide a summary of Beowulf; discuss the story and its connection to the King letter. Journal entry— 'How does Beowulf inform our lives?' Thursday: rewrite journal entries. Friday: introduce writing process. Do Venn diagram of two authors—informing our lives; review entries and discuss connection between the King letter and Beowulf."

Obviously, the second plan leaves out much that is offered in the textbook. The second plan, however, is more directly connected with the two objectives selected as a focus for the course. As the semester moves on, the teacher will ignore a lot of the literature and historic exposition in the 723-page text. As she proceeds through the course, she will select that literature which best helps the students relate literature to life as they develop their basic expository writing skills. By the end of the course, it is highly likely that these students will have a greater appreciation for, a greater understanding of, and a greater knowledge base about the required literature than they would have had, had the teacher stayed with the coverage method. In addition, by using the second core objective as a tool for communicating about the first, she will have students better able to produce a meaningful essay than if she had used the typical "fill-in-the-time" format with unconnected writing tasks.

In addition to restructuring curriculum so that less is truly more, a teacher can take advantage of the three-story model to increase the challenge level of her tasks. For instance, in the ninth grade example, the teacher might spend the first quarter of the year structuring writing assignments that require students to improve the quality of their information gathering (first story). As they read the literature and background material, she can focus their attention on the story line, facts about the characters, and settings and historical background. Practice essays will ask the students to give details and describe with facts. As the students become more precise in these tasks, she can move the written assignments to the second story by asking them to use the gathered information to compare and contrast and to explain why. In the second half of the year, the students are ready to go to the third story and respond to essay tasks which require evaluation, prediction, and synthesis.

A third use of the three-story intellect occurs when the teacher/mediator uses the model to teach students how to inquire. After posting the three-story model, she can demonstrate to the class the techniques she is using to ask questions in the discussions and in structuring their writing assignments. To make use of what they have learned about asking questions, she can use think-pair-share groups which begin with the students developing their own questions about the material they are studying. This can be as simple as allowing time at the end of each unit for pairs to structure questions about the material studied and posing them to the class.

Other Question-Asking Strategies

Question-asking strategies that challenge students can take other forms, too.

Question Web

At the end of the lesson, pair students. Each pair is to review the lesson material and form a question (what? why? when? where? or how?) about some part they don't understand or a part that is important to highlight. After all pairs have come up with a question (allow five minutes), call on students at random to provide questions. On the board or overhead, use a web to write the questions. After you have all questions (don't duplicate any), guide a discussion to answer each one. Use your own extending questions so that students have the first chance to answer.

Three-to-One Technique

Ask questions that allow at least *three* possible answers. In trios each student will give one possible answer for the recorder to write. Ask a follow-up question that challenges students to agree on the *one* best answer from the trio's list. They can rank or combine ideas. The checker checks to see if *(a)* all members agree (members signal thumbs up), *(b)* each member can explain the selected answer, and *(c)* each member can tell why that answer was selected. Members should rehearse *(b)* and *(c)* before signing the group's worksheet to indicate "I agree," "I can explain," and "I can tell why we decided on this."

Newspaper Graphic

Give each pair of students a copy of this graphic with instructions to use the completed material as the source for the format.

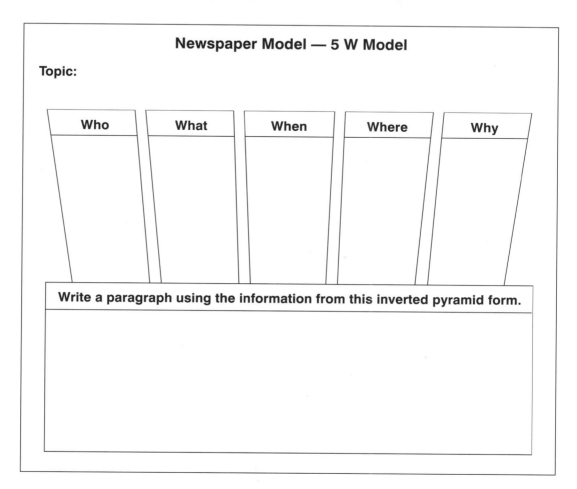

Beyond *strategies* that mediate challenge, the mediating teacher can build *lessons* that challenge students to rely on their own observations, thinking patterns, and ability to generalize in order to construct meaning and deepen understanding. Note in the following lessons how teacher/mediators have structured lessons that teach key curricular concepts (e.g., circumference, community) by starting with concrete experiences and ending with generalizations that challenge.

Problem-Solving Stories

Problem
How to read a story from a problem focus.

Focus Intelligence
Verbal/Linguistic.

Supporting Intelligences
All.

▪ CHECKING PRIOR KNOWLEDGE

Post the problem-solving observation chart for the children to review the listed behaviors. Select a strong reader to read each behavior and lead the class in a choral reading review. Indicate that you will use the chart again as you observe them practicing the behaviors during the group work for this lesson.

▪ STRUCTURING THE TASK

1. Select a story on video. (You may use this same lesson outline for several problem-solving practice lessons.) Following is a selection of story videos. Be sure to preview each one to determine the spots in the story where you want to stop and have the students discuss the questions. (You may wish to substitute a story that you read to the class. Use the same questions at the appropriate spot in each story. If you have sufficient readers, before the video or in place of the video, have a reader in each group read the story and stop at the places you indicate so that the groups can discuss the questions.)

<table>
<tr><td colspan="3" align="center">**Stories Available on Video**</td></tr>
<tr><td>• How the Elephant Got His Trunk</td><td>• The Staunch Tin Soldier</td><td>• Hansel and Gretel</td></tr>
<tr><td>• The Tinder Box</td><td>• Little Tom Thumb</td><td>• Rumpelstiltskin</td></tr>
<tr><td>• The Emperor's New Clothes</td><td>• The Frog Prince</td><td>• The Boy Who Cried Wolf</td></tr>
<tr><td>• Sleeping Beauty</td><td>• Tale of the Ugly Duckling</td><td>• The Ears of King Midas</td></tr>
</table>

2. Before you start the video, divide the class into trios. Use cards with colored dots to determine the jobs in each group. The reader will read the questions and the story, if you elect that approach; the recorder will write the answers; the checker will make sure that all members agree with each answer.

3. Give a copy of the problem-solving worksheet to each recorder:

IRI/SkyLight Training and Publishing, Inc.

Problem-Solving Worksheet

Names _____

The Problem	Ways to Solve the Problem	The Solution

4. Tell students that you will stop the video as soon as the problem or challenge is identified. Review the questions on the problem-solving observation chart that the group will use at this spot. After you have shown the video or told the story, allow five minutes for each group to fill in the first block on their problem-solving worksheet, "the problem."

5. Repeat the procedure for each of the remaining two blocks. Tell where you will stop, review the appropriate problem-solving behaviors, and allow five minutes after the video.

■ LOOKING BACK

Ask for sample responses to each of the blocks. Write the samples on the board and discuss the variations. Encourage the class to agree on a single response. Do not suggest or give an answer. Summarize what each group reports and ask for agreements. Finalize the agreement for each block on the chart before you proceed to the next one. When you are gathering the data from the groups, avoid going back to the same groups.

■ BRIDGING FORWARD

1. Invite the groups to write the following on the back of the problem-solving worksheet: (1) a lesson they learned from how the character(s) in this story solved the problem; (2) what problem-solving behaviors from the chart they used well. Sample the responses to each question. After the groups have shared their answers to the second question, use the chart to give your feedback on the problem-solving behaviors you observed. Post it for the class to see.

2. Chart the students' uses of the problem-solving behaviors so they can see their own progress. You may wish to add an incentive for the class to reach certain milestones. Use of the chart will benefit the students most if you use this same lesson outline with a sequence of stories and mediate for challenge as each story becomes more difficult.

Materials

Problem-solving observation charts, selected video, TV, video player, index cards, colored dots, problem-solving worksheet, masking tape.

Variations

1. If video equipment is not available, select a story to read to the class.

2. For "Look Back and Review," mediate challenge by asking students to discuss *(a)* the challenges faced by the story characters, *(b)* how each dealt with the challenge, and *(c)* what they could learn from the characters about "challenges."

IRI/SkyLight Training and Publishing, Inc.

MIDDLE SCHOOL LESSON

Heritage Heroes

Problem
How to benefit from the contributions made to American history by cultural groups represented in the classroom.

Focus Intelligence
Verbal/Linguistic.

Supporting Intelligence
Intrapersonal.

■ CHECKING PRIOR KNOWLEDGE

1. Create one or more webs on a bulletin board labeled "Heritage Heroes." (Make one web for each culture represented in the class.)

2. Invite students to make a name card for each famous person they can identify by name. Place it on the appropriate web. Invite students to tell what they know about the nominees.

■ STRUCTURING THE TASK

To the webs already started, add names that were not nominated.

1. Invite each student to select one name from the web. Allow one week for each student to research the person. Have them get the following information:

   a. Who is this person? (important dates and facts)

   b. What contributions did he or she make?

   c. What challenges did he or she overcome?

   d. What lessons can we learn from his or her life?

   Show students how to use index cards to record answers and identify the source of information.

2. Instruct each student to write a five-paragraph essay (one beginning, three middle, one end) that answers the questions. Discuss the indicators of success you will use. Discuss with each student the first draft and correct grammar, spelling, structure, etc.

3. Collect, review, and post the final drafts.

4. Randomly assign three students to a group. The group will identify how the different "heroes" are alike and different in their thinking, beliefs, and attitudes.

5. Give each group time to plan and produce a five-minute meeting of the "heroes" on a TV interview show. The heroes will discuss a current event. Afterwards, the group members will each explain why their characters argued for a certain point. (To allow time for this pageant, play only two to three presentations per day.)

Heritage Heroes

African Americans

Muhammad Ali
Maya Angelou
Louis Armstrong
Arthur Ashe
Marian Anderson
James Baldwin
Benjamin Banneker
Ronald Brown
William Bessie
Mary McLeod Bethune
Gwendolyn Brooks
George W. Carver
Cab Calloway
Dr. William "Bill" Cosby
Countee Cullen
Frederick Douglass
W. E. B. DuBois
Paul L. Dunbar
Charles Drew
Jean-Baptiste DuSable
Medgar Evers
Marcus Garvey
Althea Gibson
Nikki Giovanni
Lorraine Hansbury
Billie Holiday
Langston Hughes
Rev. Dr. Martin Luther King, Jr.
Thurgood Marshall
James Meredith
Garrett Morgan
Jesse Owens
Rosa Parks
Leontyne Price
Joseph Rainey
A. Phillip Randolph
Paul Robeson
Jackie Robinson
Octavia Rogers
Sojourner Truth
Harriet Tubman

Madame C. J. Walker
Ida B. Wells
Roy Wilkins
Carter G. Woodson
Malcolm X
Andrew Young

Other World Figures of African Descent

Aesop
Sonni Ali
Richmond Barthé
Ludwig van Beethoven
Robert Browning
Paul Belloni Du Chaillu
Cleopatra
Samuel Taylor Coleridge
Samuel Crowler
Alfred Dobbs
Alexandre Dumas
Hannibal
H. H. Harrison
Queen Hatshepsut
Richard Hill
Imhotep
Isaac Wallace-Johnson
Lokman
Makeda, Queen of Sheba
Nelson Mandela
Joachim Murat
Allesandro de' Medici
Queen Nzingha
Touissant L'Overture
Aleksander Pushkin
Haile Selassie
Charles Spaulding
Mary Church Terrell
Thutmose III
William Trotten
Desmond Tutu
Zenobia

Hispanic Americans

Lope de Aguirre
Pedro Antonio de Alarcón
Isaac Albéniz
Pedro de Alvarado
Everett Alvarez
Jorge Carrera Andrade
Pío Baroja
Garcia Calderon
Richard E. Cavazos
César Chávez
Roberto Clemente
Fernando De Rojas
Roberto Durán
Carlos Finlay
Fernanco García
Carlos Gomes
Cecilia Gonzalez
Guerrero
Jose Maria deHeredia
Julio Iglesias
Juan Ramón Jiménez
Agustín Lara
Diego Maradona
Ricardo Montalbán
Rita Moreno
Juan Ortega
Manuel Piar
Horacio Rivero
Chi Chi Rodriguez
César Romero
Francisco de Zorrilla Rojas
Arantxa Sanchez-Vicario
George Santayana
Lee Treviño
Fernando Valenzuela
Joseph White

Other World Figures of Hispanic Descent

Vasco Núñez de Balboa
Simón Bolívar
Jorge Luis Borges
Pablo Casals
Salvador Dalí
Plácido Domingo
Benito Juárez
Federico García Lorca
Pablo Neruda
Pelé
Pablo Picasso
Diego Rivera
Andrés Segovia
Fray Junípero Serra
Diego Velázquez
Emiliano Zapata

Native Americans

Dr. Charles Alexander
Bigfoot
Abel Bosum
Joseph Brant
Cochise
Crazy Horse/ Tashunkewitko
Dan George
Geronimo
Hurston
Joseph
Naiche
Zora Neale
Quanna Parker
Gregory Perillo
Pontiac
Red Cloud
John Ross
Santana
Sequoya
Sitting Bull
Tecumseh

IRI/SkyLight Training and Publishing, Inc.

■ LOOKING BACK

Ask the students to discuss what lessons they learned about facing challenges from the "heroes." How might they apply the same resources in facing their everyday lives?

■ BRIDGING FORWARD

Invite each student to write a letter to his character. The letter will explain what lessons the student learned and how the student will apply that lesson to his own life. Be sure to review the indicators of success before they write.

Assessing Student Performance

1. To what degree does the five-paragraph essay respond to the four questions in a clear and concise manner?

2. To what degree does the group presentation capture the beliefs and ideas of the characters?

3. To what degree does the letter make a significant application of the character's best qualities?

Materials

Bulletin board, tacks or tape, multicolored paper, markers or crayons, index cards.

Variations

1. Allow groups of three to do the research on a character.

2. Make a complete pageant with authentic costumes for each character.

3. In place of the essay, assign students to make a collage for each character.

4. In place of the current events discussion, give each group a current social problem to solve from the perspective of the "heroes." Let them enact the solution in a mini-play.

SECONDARY SCHOOL LESSON

Around and Around

Problem
How to *estimate* circumference.

Focus Intelligence
Logical/Mathematical.

Supporing Intelligences
Bodily/Kinesthetic, Visual/ Spatial, Interpersonal, Intrapersonal, Verbal/ Linguistic.

■ CHECKING PRIOR KNOWLEDGE

Invite one student from the class to determine which is greater, the circumference of a glass or its height. Give the student a sample drinking glass. After the student's "guess," ask the class to agree or disagree. Most will guess wrong and say "height." After several examples, they will begin to "estimate" with facts rather than "guesses." Solicit *reasons* for each different response. Repeat the procedure with two to three different glasses. List the methods for determining the correct answer. If no one contributes the terms "radius," "circumference," or "diameter," add them to the list and provide their definitions. Conclude by presenting the word "estimate." Ask for definitions, examples, and how knowing "circumference" and "radius" helped sharpen estimates of the glasses. Celebrate competence and prepare the students for transfer.

■ STRUCTURING THE TASKS

On the board make a map to show the connection of the key terms. Share the purpose of the lesson: "to learn how to use mathematical formulas to sharpen estimates of circular figures." Put students into trios. Assign the roles of calculator, checker, and encourager. Give each group a plastic bag containing (1) a calculator, (2) a tape measure, (3) three paper plates of different size, and (4) the worksheet. Groups will measure the radius of each plate and use the formula to calculate circumference. (Allow fifteen minutes.)

■ LOOKING BACK

Allow each group of two students to discuss these questions before you sample the total class:

1. What are your answers? How close were your estimates? What helped improve your estimates?

2. What did members of your group contribute to your team work?

IRI/SkyLight Training and Publishing, Inc.

■ BRIDGING FORWARD

For student journal entries, select one or more tasks from item 1 below:

1. Solve these word problems:

   a. What will be the circumference of wheels having the following radii: 17", 36", 7", or 129"?

   b. If you have a truck with 39" (diameter) wheels, how many times will the wheels turn in a three-mile trip? (There are _____ inches in a mile.)

   c. Read the problem and give instructions for its solution. Mary's bicycle wheels have a 39" diameter. Mary rides her bike to school each day, taking the same 4.5 mile route each way. How many times will her front wheel turn in a round trip to and from school? Instructions must include: *(a)* multiply the mileage by 2 for the round trip; *(b)* convert miles to inches; *(c)* divide 19.5" into mileage; and *(d)* calculate circumference.

   d. Invent your own circumference word problem and give instructions for its completion.

   e. Explain the terms "circumference," "diameter," and/or "radius" and tell why each is important to know.

   f. Make a list of objects in this room or your home on which you could use your math knowledge to estimate circumference. Pick one and show off your know-how.

2. After students have worked the problems, sample their work in a discussion.

Assessing Student Performance

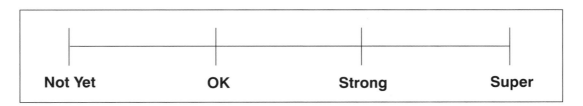

Not Yet   **OK**   **Strong**   **Super**

How well can the student:

1. explain the mathematical vocabulary and give examples from daily life of how the concepts are connected?

2. measure circular figures for radius and use the correct mathematical formula to calculate for circumference?

3. explain why knowledge of the formula is important in daily life?

Materials

Several glasses with different heights and circumferences, overhead projector and transparencies, one calculator, tape measure, plates in three different sizes, worksheet in plastic envelope, and student journals.

Variations

1. Substitute triangles, squares, or any other geometric figure. Provide models in various sizes of the figure linked to the measurement formula for hands-on work.

2. Provide home-life follow-up measurement (e.g., for circumference—dishes, storage containers, garbage cans, etc.).

CHAPTER 11

Self-Change

If you wait for tomorrow,
tomorrow comes. If you
don't wait for tomorrow,
tomorrow comes.

—Sierra Leonian proverb

This tenth criterion for mediation, *self-change*, is like the final rush of energy and effort at the end of a marathon. All the other mediations are built on the assumption that the mediator's essential responsibility is to mediate and increase students' desire to change and to change how they learn throughout life. Students' recognition, acceptance, valuing, and monitoring of change within themselves, however, is what leads them to the finish line of independent and autonomous learning.

Feuerstein argues that the ability to change is the most stable characteristic of human beings. Whether a person wants to acknowledge that change is occurring all around and within, change is always present and ongoing. Many people resist this—it is often easier to stay in a comfort zone than to ease down the road to self-change.

☐ Facilitating Self-Change

The mediator cannot force a student to change. She can help the student become aware of the dynamic potential for change. She can mediate the pluses and minuses of the change. From this awareness will come the self-control in learning that is the core of Feuerstein's work. This self-control involves the recognition that change comes from within, an expectation for growth in competence, self-monitoring for personal change, and an increased openness to helping oneself change and move through the comfort zones.

Some of the classroom strategies that are beneficial in mediating self-change are:

- elimination of labels and categories that tell students they cannot change;
- increased respect for individual talents and discouragement of comparisons among students;
- elimination of put-downs, slurs, and personal attacks;
- promotion of student self-evaluation;
- reduction of self-defeating behavior and language;
- development of an understanding of change within each student;
- use of personal standards and goals to help students guide their changes;
- increased monitoring of self through progress charts and portfolios;
- provision of helpful feedback; and
- development of self-reporting parent conferences.

Of these ten, the first four require special notice for use in the urban school.

Elimination of Change-Inhibiting Labels and Categories

American educators are first in the world with labels and categories. Their students, like animals in a zoo, are tested, prodded, grouped, and labeled. Meant to individualize education in a diagnostic-treatment mode, the labels create low-expectations, isolation, and peer umbrage rather than raise performance or achievement levels. Students, long categorized and provided with "dumbed-down" curricula, cocoon themselves with excuses and rationalizations for doing less in learning quality and quantity. Classrooms without useless labels and categories, and schools without tracks and ability groups, free students from some of the sources of low-expectations.

Respect for Individual Talent and Discouragement of Comparisons

Although much lip service is paid to individualized instruction, labeled students adapt readily to the low expectations held for them. Students with behavior disorders learn how to live up to that label by acting out; students with learning disabilities use "I don't have to do that because . . ." strategies with their teachers and parents; students at risk of failure assume a passive role with their academic work. There is little mystery to what is happening: these students are finding quick cover. Even though they may possess talents other than those used to make academic classifications, they know that their musical, visual, or interpersonal intelligences are not too highly esteemed. For survival amongst their peers, they often find it more expedient to adopt their label and perform according to their expected designation. However, when a teacher fights the systematic negation of multiple talents and multiple intelligences, she creates a classroom in which all students are respected for their individual talents. Even more, she creates a new set of expectations which challenge students to use their talents to achieve higher academic and life goals.

Elimination of Put Downs

Whenever a teacher establishes a classroom climate that celebrates individual differences, student behavior moves to a higher plane. Instead of the accepted put downs, slurs, and personal attacks which alienate students from each other, the mediating teacher is proactive in demanding verbal respect for all. This may require explicit social skill lessons, development of teamwork skills, celebrations of individual accomplishments, and public recognition of those who make extra effort to treat all peers with respect. Physical safety and security are the first right of every student in the classroom; emotional safety and security are the second. Without these foundation pieces, self-change will not begin.

> I have forgiven myself; I'll make a change. Once that forgiveness has taken place you can console yourself with the knowledge that a diamond is the result of extreme pressure. Less pressure is crystal, less than that is coal, less than that is fossilized leaves or plain dirt. Pressure can change you into something quite precious, quite wonderful, quite beautiful. . . .
> —Maya Angelou, *USA Today*, 5 March 1985

When a teacher establishes a classroom climate that celebrates individual differences, student behavior moves to a higher plane.

Promotion of Reflection and Self-Assessment

When students are raised in an environment that promotes impulsive reactions and incidental experience, young students fail to form the habits of mind that lead to high achievement. Recent brain research accentuates the value of guiding students to learn how to plan what they will do, how to monitor their own progress, and how to make judgments on the quality of their work. When these three elements apply to their thinking processes and they begin to "think about their thinking," gains on achievement are remarkable (Fogarty 1994). However, students need the time and the guidance of a teacher/mediator to develop these reflective habits.

There are a variety of strategies that provide simple yet powerful facilitation of student reflection and self-assessment. In the BUILD model of cooperative learning (Bellanca and Fogarty 1991), these strategies are described as the tools which motivate students to "look back and reflect." These looks back include *(a)* a review of what students learned in terms of facts, concepts, or insights into the curriculum and in terms of how to work successfully in a team and how to solve problems; *(b)* a review of how students learned the content and used their team building and thinking skills; and *(c)* how they might improve their learning, cooperating, and thinking dispositions. Introduced and modeled through direct instruction techniques, these strategies provide an opportunity for the mediator to extend student reflection from simple, short responses into elaborate self-assessments that encourage each student to monitor his own cognitive and affective growth.

Reflective journals are an excellent medium for continuous self-assessment. Laminated feedback cards promote select dialogue between mediator and student (see samples below). Index cards are easy to collect and review.

> Students raised in an environment that promotes impulsive reactions fail to form the habits of mind that lead to high achievement.

Feedback Card

(Side 1)	(Side 2)
Topic _____ Name_____ Student Reflects Here:	Mediator Reflects Here:

When the mediator provides the framework for student responses, she makes it easier for students to avoid writer's block and to provide increasingly more elaborate responses. Three strategies provide useful self-assessment frameworks for content, cooperation, or cognition.

IRI/SkyLight Training and Publishing, Inc.

In a conventional classroom inculcated with behaviorist practices, there is no time for student self-assessment. The teacher dispenses, judges, rewards (with stars, stickers, and high grades), and punishes (with time-outs, red ink, and low grades). In the mediated classroom, the teacher establishes performance criteria and indicators of success before key lessons. As students work, they take time to check progress against the criteria, listening to the teacher's corrective feedback on how well their work in progress matches the criteria.

Time for learning how to use reflective strategies and to build a disposition for self-assessment is a long-term task. It can begin in the primary grades in small increments with simple "I learned" stems in a wraparound. At the end of a lesson, the teacher says: "I would like each of you to take a turn saying one thing you learned in this _____ lesson. Do not repeat or copy someone else's words. Use your own idea. Listen to each other."

Patient redirection by the mediator will encourage both reflective thought and honest sharing behaviors.

"I Learned" Stems

Today, I learned that . . .

I discovered . . .

I understand why . . .

Scheduling reflective time each day will add to the benefit derived from the mediation of self-control and the mediation of sharing. Egocentric children will interrupt each other, jump out of turn, and forget about listening to others. Patient redirection by the mediator will encourage both reflective thought and honest sharing behaviors. As the students fall into a greater comfort zone with reflection, setting learning goals, and assessing their own progress, the process of individuation aproaches its zenith.

In the middle grades regular use of de Bono's PMI or Bellanca's "Mrs. Potter's Questions" provides the opportunity to develop deep reflection. Whether tying these strategies to the completion of an essay in language arts, a science experiment, a fine arts project, or a wellness challenge, the mediator structures the development of students' disposition to learn.

Mrs. Potter's Questions

What was I expected to do?	What might I change in the future?
What did I do well?	What help do I need?

PMI		
P Pluses	**M** Minuses	**I** Interesting Questions

The Mediation of Self-Change

The mediator at any grade level also can enhance self-change by structuring lessons and projects that expand their students' understanding of self-change and its benefits.

Famous People Who Have Changed Our Lives

Problem
To understand the contributions people of color have made to the history of the United States.

Focus Intelligences
Verbal/Linguistic, Visual/Spatial.

Supporting Intelligences
Interpersonal, Intrapersonal.

■ CHECKING PRIOR KNOWLEDGE

Ask the class to help you complete a KWL chart (Know, What to Know, and Learned) about famous African Americans. After the first two columns are complete, let the class know the problem they will solve in this lesson. (See above.)

■ STRUCTURING THE TASK

1. Divide the class into groups of three. Each group will select one name from the K list and three questions from the W list.

2. Provide age-appropriate print and/or video materials about each selected person. The group will use the materials: (a) to find a picture of the person; (b) to answer the questions about the person; and (c) to pick out ways that person changed his or her own life and the lives of others.

3. Using posterboard and markers or crayons, the group is to depict the before/after change experienced by this person.

4. Display the completed pictures.

■ LOOKING BACK

Make an all-class list of the various ways the featured persons made changes in their own lives. Discuss the importance of "taking charge" and changing your own life.

■ BRIDGING FORWARD

Invite each child to write a short essay telling how what they learned from the featured persons could help them complete the essay. Use the PMI chart as a self-assessment tool. Collect the essays and charts.

Assessing Student Performance

Students will identify people of color who changed their lives. Each student will:

- identify and tell one important way to change for the good; and
- write a short essay to discuss an idea learned about self-change.

Materials

Newsprint and markers (for KWL charts); books, articles, and videotapes about people of color; poster board and markers for groups; masking tape or tacks; essay paper and pencils.

Variations

1. Select a short biography about one famous person of color. Read the story to the class.

2. Direct each student to interview a person of color he or she admires. Questions should include: "Who or What are you? What do you do? How have you changed your life for the better?" Use the data to make posters.

3. Adapt the KWL chart so it represents the cultural background of the students. If the class is predominantly Hispanic, focus the KWL on famous Hispanic Americans. If there is a mixture of student cultures in the class, be sure that the KWL groups reflect the mix.

4. To use the KWL with the World Wide Web, add a D column (for Data) before the L column. What data words will help us answer the W questions?

5. For bridging forward have each child make a personal improvement goal.

6. Have each student select a person of importance, a hero or heroine, who made significant self-change. After research, students will select ways to show how the person's willingness to change carries an important message for everyone.

MIDDLE SCHOOL LESSON

Valuing Respect

Problem
How to eliminate put downs, slurs, and disrespect in the classroom.

Focus Intelligence
Interpersonal.

Supporting Intelligences
Intrapersonal, Visual/Spatial.

■ CHECKING PRIOR KNOWLEDGE

1. Divide the class into groups of three. Assign a recorder for each group. The recorder will copy your blackboard double T-chart.

Looks Like	Sounds Like	Feels Like

2. With all members contributing, each group will list three or more ideas in each column based on their experience with "disrespect" in the school. Give specific examples for each column (Looks Like—obscene gesture; Sounds Like— "nerd"; Feels Like—anger). Allow five minutes for this listing before you ask the reporters to help you construct a list on the board or newsprint with no items duplicated. After the list is composed, show two signs and ask which they believe ought to mark this list in the classroom. Encourage random volunteers (refer to the TESA strategies) to explain why. After hearing students' responses, give your reasons for "thumbs down" to disrespect.

Thumbs Up	Thumbs Down

■ STRUCTURING THE TASK

1. Keep the same groups. Instruct each group to construct a double T-chart for "respect in the classroom." (Provide a 24" x 36" piece of newsprint or poster-board per group.)

2. After the groups have finished the T-charts, invite them to make a magazine ad for "RESPECT" with ideas taken from the chart. Show sample ads that have simple, clear, and strong messages.

Looks Like	Sounds Like	Feels Like

3. Post the ads around the classroom. Select two to three ads per day for the class to brainstorm *what they like* about the ads. They may use only *respectful* responses as generated on their T-charts.

■ LOOKING BACK

After reviewing all the ads, use the double T-charts to make a class list of the ten most important respectful behaviors for this classroom. Vote by giving each student a red dot (five points), a blue dot (three points), and a yellow dot (one point). After the master list is made, each student has three votes. Tally the score for the top ten. Post the final list.

■ BRIDGING FORWARD

Ask each student to write a reflective essay. In the essay the student will discuss: *(a)* "what I have learned" about giving respect to my classmates; and *(b)* "how I can change" to show more respect.

Assessing Student Performance

To what degree:

- can the student identify three to five respectful behaviors?
- can the student explain why respect is important?
- can the student demonstrate improvements in respect within the classroom?

Materials

Newsprint or posterboard, markers or crayons.

Variations

1. Replace the group-made ads with other media (such as essays, video, home page design, game, collage, rap song).
2. Allow each group to select its product.
3. Make the products a home assignment.
4. Hold an exhibition of the products for parents and/or other classes.
5. Use Aretha Franklin's "R-E-S-P-E-C-T" song; change the words to apply to the information generated on the double T-charts, and then perform it.

SECONDARY SCHOOL LESSON

Reflective Journals

Problem
How to introduce students to reflective thinking as a process to manage self-change.

Focus Intelligence
Intrapersonal.

Supporting Intelligence
Individual to each student.

■ CHECKING PRIOR KNOWLEDGE

1. On the overhead or with a handout, show Nikki Giovanni's (poet and children's book author) "The Funeral of Martin Luther King, Jr.":

The Funeral of Martin Luther King, Jr.

His heads she said
Free at last, Free at last
But death is a slave's freedom
We seek the freedom of free man
And the construction of a world
Where Martin Luther King could have lived
and preached non violence.—Atlanta, 4-9-68

2. Using TESA strategies (see Chapter 6) that encourage all to participate, ask this sequence of questions (ask one student to list the responses on the board):

   • In your own words, what does this poem say?

   • In what ways does this poem connect you to what you already know about Dr. King?

   • What new or different ideas and feelings does the poem stir?

■ STRUCTURING THE TASK

1. Provide each student with a journal. (This can be 20–30 stapled blank pages, a purchased notebook, or looseleaf pages at the back of a class notes binder. It is a book that you want students to bring daily or to keep in the classroom.)

2. Explain the purpose of the journal— to enable them: (a) to think deeply about the material/content they are learning in this class (yes, a math journal, science journal, art journal, as well as English journal); (b) to think how they might apply what they are learning; (c) to understand how the course content ties together; and (d) to see how they are making continuous improvement.

3. Provide the standard and criteria that you will use in reviewing the journal. You will have to decide what criteria you want for quantity (daily entry?), quality of thoughtfulness, completeness of responses, spelling and grammar requirements, etc. Provide a rubric or scale if you intend to grade the journal.

4. Explain "confidentiality." At times you will read private entries; at other times, you will call on volunteers to share their ideas with the class. Ask that the volunteers share their entries with you before they share them with the class.

5. Let students know that you will provide a structure for each entry. If they elect to make additional entries, allow them an open structure.

6. Start with the three question structure used for the poem above. If you teach in the arts or English, entries will best be made before class discussion.

   • In your own words, what does this _____ say?

   • In what ways does it connect you to what you already know about _____ ?

   • What new or different ideas or feelings does the _____ stir?

   If you teach math, science, social studies, or other courses, follow the same sequence after students have viewed or read introductory material.

   • In your own words, what does this information say?

   • What do you already know about this topic?

   • What do you predict you might be learning new or different?

7. After time is given for entries, you may wish to ask several volunteers to share responses to each question (this is a good time to practice appropriate mediation skills!).

8. A second time to use the reflective journal is at the end of a lesson or unit. Again provide "stems" to prompt the students' reflections. Be sure to remind students that you prefer *thoughtful* responses over the quick answers that they might think you want to hear. Here is a basic three-cue sequence:

   • I learned (today, in this lesson, in this unit) . . .

   • This information is important because . . .

   • To use this information (skill), I intend . . .

■ LOOKING BACK

After students have made several entries in their journals, ask them to review what they have written and write entries:

• In my entries, I am please that I . . .

• In my entries, I think I can improve by . . .

• In future entries, I intend to . . .

■ BRIDGING FORWARD

At the back of the journal, invite students to construct a course concept map. As the course progresses, have students reflect on the connections among the course topics, subtopics, and facts and create the map. Show them an example while reminding them that each map will be unique.

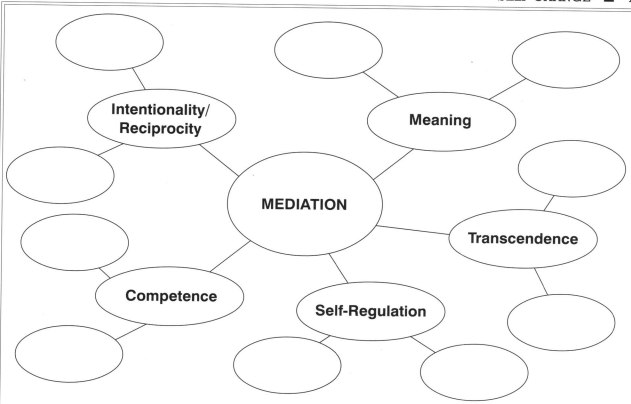

Assessing Student Performance

To what degree does the student:

- use multiple sentence responses to each cue?
- individuate her responses?
- communicate an understanding of the material?
- show continuous improvement in mastery of the course content?
- edit her verbal responses?

Materials

A journal and pencils or pens for each student.

Variations

1. Depending upon the interaction(s) you want most to mediate, review the chapter and design appropriate entries. For instance, if you want to stress *meaning* you can have students use appropriate graphic organizers with your course content. If *sharing behavior* is important for a class, focus your reflection on cues on the group process and social skills.

2. Encourage students to use a variety of media that fit individuated intelligences, especially as unique entries. Poems, songs, sketches, etc. are welcome!

3. Teach Mrs. Potter's Questions and end each week with a journal entry that assesses one area of the students' class lives: content, cooperation, cognition.

Bibliography

Anderson, Kamili. 1989. Urban coalition encourages minority youth to "say yes" to math and science. *Black Issues in Higher Education* 5(21): 6–8.

Anyon, J. 1995. Race, social class, and educational reform in an inner-city school. *Teachers College Record* 97(1): 69–94.

Apple, M. W. 1991. The politics of curriculum and teaching. *NASSP Bulletin* 75(532): 39–50.

Aronson, E. 1978. *The jigsaw classroom.* Beverly Hills, Calif.: Sage Publications.

Ascher, C. 1993. Changing schools for urban students: The school development program, accelerated schools, and success for all. *Trends and Issues No. 18.* ERIC Clearinghouse on Urban Education: New York, N. Y.

Atwater, M. M., et al. 1995. A study of urban middle school students with high and low attitudes toward science. *Journal of Research in Science Teaching* 32(6): 665–77.

Ausubel, D. 1978. *Educational psychology: A cognitive view.* 2nd ed. New York: Holt, Rinehart & Winston.

Ball, A. F. 1995. Text design patterns in the writing of urban African American students: Teaching to the cultural strengths of students in multicultural settings. *Urban Education* 30(3): 253–89.

Banathy, B. 1991. *Systems design of education: A journey to create the future.* Englewood Cliffs, N. J.: E. T. Press.

Becum, L. C., et. al. 1989. The urban landscape: Education for the twenty-first century. *Journal of Negro Education* 58(3): 430–41.

Bellanca, J., and R. Fogarty. 1991. *Blueprints for thinking in the cooperative classroom.* Arlington Heights, Ill.: IRI/SkyLight Training and Publishing.

Ben-Hur, M., ed. 1994. *On Feuerstein's Instrumental Enrichment: A collection.* Arlington Heights, Ill.: IRI/SkyLight Training and Publishing.

Brookover, W., et al. 1982. *Creating effective schools: An inservice program for enhancing school learning climate and achievement.* Holmes Beach, Flor.: Learning Publications, Inc.

Carter, R. L. 1995. The unending struggle for equal educational opportunity. *Teachers' College Record* 96(4): 619–26.

Chapman, C. 1993. *If the shoe fits . . .: How to develop multiple intelligences in the classroom.* Arlington Heights, Ill.: IRI/SkyLight Training and Publishing.

Cohen, E. 1986. *Designing groupwork: Strategies for the heterogeneous classroom.* New York: Teachers College Press.

Cohen, M. 1993, April. Patterns of school change. Paper presented at the Annual Meeting of the American Educational Research Association, Atlanta, Ga., April 1993.

Cooper, E. J., and J. Sherk. 1989. Addressing urban school reform: Issues and alliances. *Journal of Negro Education* 58(3): 315–31.

Costa, A. L., and R. Garmston. The art of cognitive coaching: Supervision for intelligence teaching. Paper presented at the Annual Conference of the Association for Supervision and Curriculum Development, Chicago, Ill., March 1985.

Cziko, C. 1995. Dialogue journals: Passing notes the academic way. *Quarterly of the National Writing Project and the Center for the Study of Writing and Literacy* 17(4): 1–5, 11.

Dahl, K. L. 1995. Challenges in understanding the learner's perspective. *Theory into Practice* 34(2): 124–30.

Dahl, K. L. and P. A. Freppon. 1995. A comparison of innercity children's interpretations of reading and writing instruction in the early grades in skills-based and whole language classrooms. *Reading Research Quarterly* 30(1): 50–74.

Davis, B. 1995. *How to involve parents in a multicultural school.* Alexandria, Va: Association for Supervision and Curriculum Development.

de Bono, E. 1985. *Six thinking hats.* Boston: Little, Brown.

Deutsch, M. 1949. An experimental study of the effects of cooperation and competition upon group processes. *Human Relations* 2: 199–232.

Dewey, J. 1933. *How we think.* Boston: D.C. Heath & Co.

Eisner, E. W. 1983. The kind of schools we need. *Educational Leadership* March, 48–55.

Feuerstein, R. 1980. *Instrumental Enrichment.* Baltimore: University Park Press.

Flavell, J. 1976. Metacognitive aspects of problem solving. In *The nature of intelligence,* edited by L. B. Resnick. Hillsdale, N.J.: Lawrence Erlbaum Associates.

Fogarty, R. 1989. From training to transfer. The role of creativity in the adult learner. Doctoral dissertation, Loyola University of Chicago.

Fogarty, R., D. Perkins, and J. Barell. 1992. *The mindful school: How to teach for transfer.* Arlington Heights, Ill.: IRI/Skylight Training and Publishing.

Frymier, J., et. al. 1992. Growing up is risky business, and schools are not to blame. Final Report, Phi Delta Kappa Study of Students At Risk. Vol. 1. Phi Delta Kappa: Bloomington, Ind.

Fullan, M., and S. Stigelbauer. 1991. *The new meaning of educational change*. New York: Teachers' College Press.

Gardner, H. 1983. *Frames of mind: The theory of multiple intelligences*. New York: Basic Books.

Glasser, W. 1986. *Control theory in the classroom*. New York: Harper & Row.

Gonzales, M. R. Multicultural education in practice: Teacher's social constructions and classroom enactments. Paper presented at the Annual Meeting of the American Educational Research Association, San Francisco, Calif., April 1995.

Goodlad J. I. 1984. *A place called school: Prospect for the future*. New York: McGraw-Hill.

Gottlieb, J., et. al. 1994. Special education in urban America: It's not justifiable for many. *Journal of Special Education* 27(4): 453–65.

Grubb, W. N. Reconstructing urban schools with work-centered education. *Education and Urban Society* 27(3): 244–59.

Harris, J. J., III, and D. Y. Ford. 1991. Identifying and nurturing the promise of gifted black American children. *Journal of Negro Education* 60(1): 3–18.

Harris, H. W., et al. 1995. *Racial and ethnic identity: Psychological development and creative expression*. New York, NY: Routledge.

Hendricks-Lee, M. S., et al. 1995. Sustaining reform through teaching learning. *Language Arts* 72(4): 288–92.

Hunter, M. 1982. *Teaching for transfer*. El Segundo, Calif.: Tip Publications.

Iwaszkiewicz, S. M. 1995. Gunfire in the night. *English Journal* 84(7): 82–83.

Jackson, M., et. al. 1991. Class, caste and the classroom: Effective public policy vs. effective public education. *Western Journal of Black Studies* 15(4): 242–47.

Jenlink, P. M., ed. 1995. *Systemic change: Touchstones for the future school*. Arlington Heights, Ill.: IRI/SkyLight Training and Publishing.

Johnson, D. W., and R. Johnson. 1986. *Circles of learning: Cooperating in the classroom*. Alexandria, Va.: Association for Supervision and Curriculum Development.

Johnson, J. A. Life after death: Critical pedagogy in an urban classroom. *Harvard Educational Review* 65(2): 213–30.

Johnson, V. R. 1990. Schools reaching out: Changing the message to "good news." *Equity and Choice* 6(3): 20–24.

Joyce, B. R., and B. Showers. 1983. *Power in staff development through research and training*. Alexandria, Va.: Association for Supervision and Curriculum Development.

Kagan, S. 1977. Social motives and behaviors of Mexican American and Anglo American Children. In *Chicano Psychology*, edited by J. L. Martinez. New York: Academic Press.

IRI/SkyLight Training and Publishing, Inc.

———. 1992. *Cooperative learning.* San Juan Capistrano, Calif.: Resources for Teachers, Inc.

King, S. H., and T. M. Bey. 1995. The need for urban teacher mentors: Conceptions and realities. *Education and Urban Society* 28(1): 3–10.

Kohn, A. 1993. *Punished by rewards.* New York: Houghton-Mifflin.

Kozol, J. 1991. *Savage inequalities.* New York: Crown.

———. 1992. Inequality and the will to change. *Equity and Choice* 8(3): 45–47.

Lee, C. D. 1995. A culturally based cognitive apprenticeship: Teaching African American high school students skills in literary interpretation. *Reading Research Quarterly* 30(4): 608–30.

Lundquist, S. 1995. The urban partnership program: A new model for strengthening communities through educational change. *Community College Journal* 65(7): 28–32.

Luria, A. R. 1976. *Cognitive development: Its cultural and social foundations.* Cambridge, Mass.: Harvard University Press.

Lyman, F., and J. McTighe. 1988. Cueing thinking in the classroom: The promise of theory embedded tools. *Educational Leadership* 45 (April): 7.

Marcus, S. A., and P. McDonald. 1990. *Tools for the cooperative classroom.* Arlington Heights, Ill.: IRI/SkyLight Training and Publishing.

National Center for Effective Schools. 1993. *Multiple intelligences theory in action: Research and the classroom.* Madison, Wis.: University of Wisconsin–Madison.

Noddings, N. 1993. For all its children. *Educational Theory* 43(1): 15–22.

Raiser, L. and S. Hinson. 1995. Writing plays using creative problem-solving. *Teaching Exceptional Children* 27(4): 59–64.

Sarason, S. B. 1990. *The predictable failure of educational reform: Can we change course before it's too late?* San Francisco: Jossey-Bass.

Schmuck, R., and P. Schmuck. 1988. *Group processes in the classroom.* Dubuque, Ia.: Wm. C. Brown.

Senge, P. 1990. *The fifth discipline: The art and practice of the learning organization.* New York: Doubleday.

Sharan, S., and Y. Sharan. 1976. *Small-group teaching.* Englewood Cliffs, N.J.: Educational Technology Publications.

———. 1992. *Expanding cooperative learning through group investigation.* New York: Teachers' College Press.

Sharron, H. 1987. *Changing children's minds: Feuerstein's revolution in the teaching of intelligecnes.* London: Souvenir Press.

Slavin, R. E. 1983. *Cooperative learning.* New York: Longman.

Sperling, M. 1995. Uncovering the role in writing and learning to write: One day in an inner-city classroom. *Written Communication* 12(1): 93–133.

Vygotsky, L. S. 1962. *Thought and language.* Cambridge, Mass.: Institute of Technology Press.

Index

IRI/SkyLight Training and Publishing, Inc.

We Prepare Your Teachers Today
for the Classrooms of Tomorrow

Learn from Our Books and from Our Authors!

Ignite Learning in Your School or District.

SkyLight's team of classroom-experienced consultants can help you foster systemic change for increased student achievement.

Professional development is a process, not an event. SkyLight's seasoned practitioners drive the creation of our on-site professional development programs, graduate courses, research-based publications, interactive video courses, teacher-friendly training materials, and online resources—call SkyLight Training and Publishing Inc. today.

SkyLight specializes in three professional development areas.

Specialty #
Best Practices

We **model** the best practices that result in improved student performance and guided applications.

Specialty #
Making the Innovations Last

We help set up **support** systems that make innovations part of everyday practice in the long-term systemic improvement of your school or district.

Specialty #
How to Assess the Results

We prepare your school leaders to encourage and **assess** teacher growth, **measure** student achievement, and **evaluate** program success.

Contact the SkyLight team and begin a process toward long-term results.

2626 S. Clearbrook Dr., Arlington Heights, IL 60005
800-348-4474 • 847-290-6600 • FAX 847-290-6609
http://www.iriskylight.com

There are
one-story intellects,
two-story intellects, and three-story
intellects with skylights. All fact collectors, who
have no aim beyond their facts, are one-story men. Two-story men
compare, reason, generalize, using the labors of the fact collectors as
well as their own. Three-story men idealize, imagine,
predict—their best illumination comes from
above, through the skylight.
—*Oliver Wendell*
Holmes

SkyLight
Training and Publishing Inc.